ABDELLATIF RAJI

Amazon KDP Algorithm

Genres, Formats, and Key Success Factors

First edition

ISBN (paperback): 978-1-963876-62-8
ISBN (hardcover): 978-1-963876-61-1
ISBN (digital): 978-1-963876-60-4

This book was professionally typeset by Yaraak.
Find out more at yaraak.com

To my family, whose unwavering support and encouragement made this endeavor possible.
To the countless readers and independent authors who continue to shape the evolving landscape of digital publishing.
And to all those who believe in the transformative power of knowledge and persistence.

"The books that the world calls immoral are books that show the world its own shame."

— Oscar Wilde

Contents

Foreword   iv

Preface   v

Acknowledgments   vi

Prologue   1

Introduction   2

I   Top Genres and Subgenres Favored by KDP Algorithms

1   Market Gravity   7

2   Knowledge Sells   11

3   Algorithmic Tides   16

4   The Power of Clustering   21

II   Format Preferences and Format-Based Promotion Patterns

5   Digital Dominance   29

6   The Strategic Value of Print   34

7   Exclusivity for Exposure   39

8   Format-Specific Promotion   44

9   Multi-Format Synergy   48

III Writing Style and Story Structure that Engage the Algorithm

10 Engagement Over Elegance   55
11 Hooked from Page One   60
12 Compounding Visibility   64
13 Writing to Market   68
14 Consistency as Strategy   73

IV Metadata, Keywords, and Categories for Discoverability

15 Metadata is the Infrastructure   81
16 Smart Targeting   85
17 Strategic Positioning   90
18 Metadata for Maximum Reach   94
19 From Indexed to Ranked   99

V Market Trends and Topics Influencing Recommendations

20 Writing to Market vs. Chasing Trends   105
21 Navigating the Trend Currents   109
22 Market-Driven Non-Fiction   114
23 Harnessing Seasonal and Niche Trends   119
24 Responding to the Market: External Trends, Viral Influence,... 124
25 Longevity vs. Flash-in-the-Pan   129

VI Reviews, Sales Velocity, Pricing, and Cover Design – Algorithmic Impacts

26 Reviews and Ratings   137
27 Sales Velocity and Launch Momentum   142

28 Pricing Strategy   147
29 Conversion Rate vs. Per-Sale Value   152
30 Promotional Pricing   157
31 KDP Select Global Fund (KU) and Pricing   162
32 Dynamic Pricing and Testing   166
33 Cover Design and Click-Through Rate   171
34 Cover and Conversion   176
35 Genre Targeting with Cover   181
36 Beyond the Cover   186

VII   Algorithm-Driven Publishing: Mastering the
Evidence-Based Strategies Behind Amazon KDP Success

37 Amazon KDP Algorithm   193
38 Evidence-Based Publishing   199
39 Mastering the Amazon KDP Ecosystem   203

40 Conclusion   208
Epilogue   210
Afterword   212
Sources   214
About the Author   215

Foreword

In an age where traditional publishing gatekeepers no longer hold exclusive power over what reaches the public eye, the rise of digital self-publishing has radically redefined the literary landscape. Amazon Kindle Direct Publishing (KDP) stands at the center of this transformation, providing a platform that empowers authors not only to publish their work but to control its production, marketing, and commercial trajectory.

This volume serves as both a guide and a critical examination of the factors that shape success in the KDP ecosystem. It draws on data-driven insights, industry practices, and algorithmic behaviors to explain how books are categorized, discovered, and promoted in the world's largest online marketplace. Whether the reader is a new author navigating the complexities of metadata, or a seasoned publisher refining a market strategy, the work offers a rigorous, systematic understanding of what drives visibility, engagement, and sales on the KDP platform.

The democratization of publishing has brought unprecedented opportunities—but also new challenges. Navigating Amazon's algorithms requires not only creativity and persistence, but strategic knowledge grounded in evidence. This book meets that need with clarity, depth, and authority.

It is a timely and necessary contribution to the scholarship and practice of independent publishing.

— *Abdellatif Raji*
Founder & CEO at Yaraak Publishing House

Preface

This work originated from a convergence of academic inquiry and practical necessity. As the landscape of publishing continues to evolve at an unprecedented pace, the mechanisms through which books are discovered, marketed, and consumed have shifted dramatically—none more influential than Amazon's Kindle Direct Publishing (KDP) platform. With over a million new titles released annually via KDP, the marketplace has become both an opportunity and a puzzle for contemporary authors.

The central aim of this book is to demystify the factors that govern visibility and success on Amazon's platform, drawing upon empirical analysis, publishing theory, and industry best practices. While algorithmic recommendation systems, reader behavior patterns, and metadata optimization are often discussed in disparate circles, this volume seeks to synthesize these domains into a coherent framework for understanding how books gain traction—and why some fail to do so.

Throughout the research and writing process, I have consulted with independent authors, digital marketers, and publishing professionals. Their contributions, direct or indirect, have informed the structure and substance of this work. This book is not a manual in the narrow sense; rather, it is a scholarly investigation with practical applications, aimed at equipping readers with the critical tools necessary to navigate a competitive digital ecosystem.

It is my hope that this book will serve not only as a resource for aspiring and established authors but also as a reference point for scholars interested in the intersection of digital platforms, content economies, and the evolving role of the author.

— *Abdellatif Raji*

Acknowledgments

This work could not have been realized without the support, insight, and encouragement of numerous individuals and institutions.

I extend my deepest gratitude to the independent authors, digital publishers, and industry professionals who generously shared their experiences and expertise throughout the research process. Their practical knowledge and candid reflections were invaluable in shaping the empirical foundation of this book.

I am particularly indebted to my academic mentors and colleagues, whose intellectual rigor and constructive critique helped refine both the methodology and the theoretical framing of this work. Their guidance served not only to challenge assumptions but also to elevate the quality of the final product.

Special thanks are due to the research librarians and data analysts who assisted in locating and interpreting key sources related to Amazon's platform metrics and publishing trends. Their contributions ensured that the analysis was both current and methodologically sound.

On a personal note, I would like to acknowledge my family for their unwavering patience and support during the extended periods of writing and revision. Their belief in the value of independent scholarship sustained me throughout the process.

Finally, to the broader community of self-publishers and readers: your commitment to democratizing knowledge and expanding access to literature continues to inspire the work that follows.

— *Abdellatif Raji*

Prologue

The 21st-century author faces a paradoxical condition: unprecedented access to the mechanisms of publication, coupled with unprecedented competition for visibility. With the advent of Amazon Kindle Direct Publishing, the literary gatekeeping of the past has given way to an algorithmically mediated marketplace in which success is no longer determined solely by literary merit, but by discoverability, reader engagement, and platform optimization.

This transformation marks a profound shift not only in publishing economics but in the very ontology of authorship. Writers are now expected to navigate metadata taxonomies, pricing strategies, keyword indexing, and marketing funnels—tasks once managed by teams of editors, marketers, and publicists. The result is a redefinition of what it means to be an author: part artist, part entrepreneur, part algorithmic analyst.

This book emerges from that intersection. It does not lament the changes brought about by digital publishing; rather, it interrogates them. It seeks to understand the logics that underlie Amazon's algorithmic systems, to identify the genres and strategies that succeed within them, and to equip authors and scholars alike with a critical framework for operating within this evolving landscape.

In what follows, the reader will find not merely tactics for commercial viability, but a deeper analysis of the digital forces that now shape literary culture. For to publish today is to enter into a dialogue not just with readers, but with machines—machines that decide who reads what, when, and why.

Introduction

In recent decades, the proliferation of digital technologies has radically transformed the means by which literary and scholarly works are produced, disseminated, and consumed. At the forefront of this transformation stands Amazon's Kindle Direct Publishing (KDP) platform—a self-publishing infrastructure that enables authors to bypass traditional gatekeepers and engage directly with a global audience. This paradigm shift, however, does not imply a disintermediation of control; rather, it replaces institutional selection processes with algorithmic curation, positioning computational systems as the new arbiters of visibility and commercial success.

This book undertakes a critical and systematic examination of the structures that govern success on Amazon KDP. It does so through an interdisciplinary lens, integrating insights from publishing studies, algorithmic culture, digital marketing, and user behavior analytics. Its central thesis is that while the democratization of publishing has lowered barriers to entry, it has simultaneously introduced new forms of competitive opacity—chief among them, the algorithmic mechanisms that regulate discovery, recommendation, and ranking within the Amazon ecosystem.

Chapter One outlines the evolution of KDP and the broader context of self-publishing within the digital economy. Chapter Two investigates the genres and subgenres most favored by Amazon's algorithmic engines, considering both historical sales data and emergent reader trends. Chapter Three explores the interplay between metadata optimization—titles, keywords, categories, and descriptions—and algorithmic indexing, offering a taxonomy of discoverability. Chapter Four considers the role of user engagement metrics—reviews, sales velocity, pricing, and Kindle Unlimited page reads—in shaping algorithmic visibility. Chapter Five examines market responsiveness and the life cycle of trends, offering a critical discussion of writing "to market" and the implications for literary diversity and sustainability.

Throughout this analysis, the book maintains a dual commitment: to equip practitioners (authors, publishers, marketers) with empirically grounded strategies for success, and to contribute to the scholarly understanding of how algorithmic infrastructures mediate cultural production. By drawing on both qualitative and quantitative methodologies, it seeks to illuminate the forces that make certain texts rise and others vanish within the vast digital sea of self-published literature.

Ultimately, this work argues that success on KDP is neither wholly meritocratic nor entirely arbitrary; it is contingent—shaped by the confluence of human creativity, reader behavior, market dynamics, and machine learning systems. Understanding this confluence is not only a practical imperative for today's authors but also a theoretical necessity for scholars of contemporary publishing.

I

Top Genres and Subgenres Favored by KDP Algorithms

"Top Genres and Subgenres Favored by KDP Algorithms"
explores how Amazon's system naturally elevates high-demand
genres like romance, thrillers, and self-help through data-driven
visibility. "Market Gravity" refers to how popular genres attract
more readers and sales, pulling similar books into orbit.
"Knowledge Sells" highlights the strength of evergreen
non-fiction categories where readers seek value and expertise.
"Algorithmic Tides" captures the ebb and flow of trend-driven
subgenres—such as mafia romance or academy fantasy—that rise
rapidly when demand spikes. Finally, "The Power of
Clustering" reveals how Amazon's algorithm groups similar
books through reader behavior, reinforcing visibility within
tightly defined niches.

Top Genres and Subgenres Favored by KDP Algorithms

1

Market Gravity

Why Romance and Thrillers Dominate Amazon's KDP Rankings

In the ecosystem of Amazon's Kindle Direct Publishing (KDP), where digital content is governed by algorithmic responsiveness to consumer behavior, certain literary genres emerge as gravitational centers. Chief among these are **romance** and **thrillers**, including the closely related crime and mystery subgenres. These categories, by virtue of consistent high-volume sales and reader loyalty, do not merely perform well—they exert a self-reinforcing influence on Amazon's recommendation systems, category rankings, and promotional features. In other words, **they dominate because they sell, and they continue to sell because they dominate**.

From the perspective of Amazon's algorithms, visibility is not granted based on artistic merit or novelty but rather on **transactional performance**. A book that rapidly accumulates sales, borrows through Kindle Unlimited, and reader engagement—manifested in reviews, completions, and series read-through—signals value to the platform. Thus, genres that consistently attract high reader engagement naturally gain **algorithmic favor**, being recommended more often and ranking more prominently across the Kindle

Store's search results and bestseller charts.

The Romance Engine

Romance, particularly, serves as a cornerstone of KDP profitability and algorithmic circulation. This genre boasts one of the **most voracious and prolific readerships** in contemporary digital publishing. Romance readers are not passive consumers—they are **habitual purchasers**, frequently consuming multiple titles per week. This behavior translates to **rapid and sustained sales velocity**, a core metric in Amazon's best-seller rank (BSR) algorithm. Furthermore, the genre lends itself naturally to **serialization**, with authors publishing expansive interconnected series that fuel ongoing reader engagement. As a result, romance novels benefit from strong "read-through" rates: readers who finish Book One often immediately purchase Book Two, and so forth, creating cascading sales patterns that the algorithm recognizes and rewards.

Moreover, romance novels are structurally suited to Kindle Unlimited (KU), Amazon's subscription-based reading platform. Because KU payouts are based on pages read (measured via Kindle Edition Normalized Page Count or KENP), **longer romance novels with compelling pacing**—which encourage binge-reading—garner higher payouts and push those titles into KU bestseller lists. Enrolling a romance novel in KDP Select (thus enabling KU access) often dramatically enhances its visibility and discoverability, particularly among the genre's existing subscriber base.

The Thrill Factor: Crime, Mystery, and Suspense

Alongside romance, **thrillers—particularly crime and mystery fiction—rank among the most consistently high-performing genres on Amazon**. Their enduring popularity derives from their **broad demographic appeal** and **cross-cultural narrative archetypes**. Readers of suspenseful fiction demonstrate strong brand loyalty, not merely to authors but to recurring protagonists and investigative frameworks (e.g., detective series, legal thrillers). These genre conventions support **episodic storytelling**, making thriller series highly effective in capturing repeat purchases. Just as with romance, the algorithm identifies these consumption loops and reinforces them through "Customers Also Bought" recommendations and direct emails to prior buyers.

Thrillers also benefit from **international appeal** and adaptation flexibility. Given their often plot-driven narratives and high stakes, they translate well across languages and resonate with global audiences. As Amazon operates in multiple marketplaces, genres with transnational appeal gain a comparative advantage. In algorithmic terms, books that perform well in multiple geographic markets accumulate more sales velocity and receive cross-marketplace exposure.

Algorithmic Feedback Loops

What distinguishes these two genres in the KDP landscape is the degree to which **reader behavior aligns with Amazon's algorithmic priorities**. When readers demonstrate rapid and consistent purchasing behavior, high engagement rates, and frequent reviews within a genre, Amazon's systems register that as market momentum. The result is a **feedback loop**:

1. Books in romance and thriller categories receive more visibility due to their historical performance.
2. This increased visibility drives more sales.
3. More sales improve rank and recommendation frequency.
4. High-ranking titles are promoted further, via homepage placements, bestseller lists, and email campaigns.

This loop creates a form of **algorithmic lock-in**, where the genres that have succeeded in the past are those most likely to succeed in the future. For new authors entering the market, this dynamic can serve as both an opportunity and a limitation. Writing within a high-demand genre like romance or thriller offers a **higher probability of discoverability**, but also demands precise adherence to genre conventions and reader expectations to remain competitive.

Conclusion

In sum, the structural dynamics of Amazon KDP's marketplace are not genre-agnostic. Rather, they reflect and amplify consumer preferences through data-driven algorithms that elevate high-performing genres. **Romance and thrillers dominate not by accident, but because they continually deliver the behavioral metrics Amazon's system is designed to reward**: frequent purchases, consistent engagement, and high retention. For authors seeking to optimize their visibility and revenue on the platform, aligning with these genre ecosystems can offer a strategic advantage—provided they are prepared to meet the expectations of a well-trained and highly discerning audience.

2

Knowledge Sells

The Rise of Non-Fiction Bestsellers in Amazon's KDP Marketplace

In the evolving digital publishing landscape of Amazon Kindle Direct Publishing (KDP), non-fiction has emerged as a formidable counterpart to fiction, not only rivaling but, in many cases, **surpassing it in sales volume**. Contrary to the assumption that Kindle readers are primarily fiction enthusiasts, a deep examination of recent e-book sales data reveals that **non-fiction categories regularly top the charts**, commanding a significant share of both revenue and reader engagement.

Genres such as **Religion & Spirituality**, **Biographies & Memoirs**, **Business & Money**, and **Self-Help** have established themselves as dominant verticals within the Kindle ecosystem. These categories, traditionally robust in print, have adapted with exceptional success to the digital medium. Their consistent sales performance signals a broader trend: **readers are increasingly turning to Kindle not just for entertainment but for knowledge acquisition and personal development**.

Self-Help and Business: High-Converting Niches

Among the most commercially successful segments within non-fiction are **self-help** and **business** titles. These books appeal to a readership motivated by improvement—whether in health, wealth, productivity, or mindset. This intrinsic utility drives demand and translates to **strong sales conversion rates**. When a reader searches for a solution—be it "how to invest in real estate" or "how to overcome anxiety"—they are often **in a buying mindset**, seeking immediate, actionable information. In marketing terms, these are *high-intent customers*, and KDP's algorithm rewards books that satisfy this intent by elevating their visibility in search and recommendation feeds.

Self-help books in particular benefit from being **highly nicheable**, enabling authors to target sub-markets with surgical precision. Titles addressing specific problems (e.g., social anxiety, habit formation, morning routines) are more likely to rank well for targeted keyword searches, especially when paired with compelling titles and well-structured metadata. Furthermore, these books often have long tails—steady sales over time due to the **evergreen nature of human self-improvement**—which aligns favorably with Amazon's algorithmic preferences for consistency and longevity in sales patterns.

Business books, especially those centered on entrepreneurship, investing, marketing, and passive income strategies, also enjoy **strong, recurrent demand**. These titles are often priced higher than fiction, yet readers perceive them as **investments** rather than discretionary purchases. As such, KDP authors who publish well-researched, clearly positioned business titles frequently report **rapid early sales**, making them algorithmically attractive during the critical "Hot New Releases" period. The strategic inclusion of case studies, frameworks, and calls to action further enhances reader retention—an important signal for Amazon's systems.

Biographies, Memoirs, and Spirituality: Emotion and Meaning

While self-help and business titles appeal to rational utility, categories like **Biographies & Memoirs** and **Religion & Spirituality** engage the reader on a more **emotional or existential level**. The former leverages narrative-driven authenticity, often appealing through storytelling that resonates across cultural, political, or inspirational lines. The latter meets a perennial human need for meaning, moral orientation, and transcendence. These genres often exhibit **strong review performance**, as readers compelled by personal stories or spiritual insight are more likely to leave thoughtful feedback—a factor that feeds directly into Amazon's algorithmic assessment of a book's credibility and quality.

Importantly, memoirs and spiritual books tend to perform well when marketed with a **distinct authorial voice or public profile**. KDP authors who cultivate a personal brand—through blogging, podcasting, or public speaking—can create a funnel of loyal readers who view their e-books not just as content but as extensions of a broader intellectual or spiritual journey. When these readers convert in sufficient volume, Amazon's system elevates the book via "Customers Also Bought" recommendations and high placement in niche categories such as *Christian Living, Eastern Philosophy,* or *Inspirational Memoirs.*

Algorithmic Alignment with Non-Fiction Content

What makes non-fiction genres especially potent in the KDP environment is their **natural alignment with Amazon's algorithmic structure**. These books often:

- Contain **search-optimized titles** (e.g., *"How to Retire at 40", "Intermittent Fasting for Women Over 50"*),
- Generate **high click-through and conversion rates** due to urgency

and utility,

- Achieve **steady sales velocity**, especially when tied to evergreen topics,
- Elicit **engaged reviews**, reinforcing trust signals to both readers and the algorithm.

Moreover, non-fiction is typically **less vulnerable to market saturation** than fiction. While genre fiction can become crowded with trend-chasing titles, a non-fiction book that offers unique insight or practical value retains its relevance longer. The algorithm recognizes this sustained interest, often maintaining visibility for non-fiction titles well beyond the typical promotional lifecycle.

Strategic Implications for KDP Authors

For independent authors seeking to maximize reach and profitability on Amazon, targeting high-demand non-fiction categories presents a strategic opportunity. The key lies in **content precision, metadata optimization, and audience alignment**. Successful non-fiction authors often conduct rigorous keyword research, select low-competition subcategories, and ensure their book titles function both as **solutions to problems** and as **compelling marketing hooks**.

The non-fiction market rewards those who can blend **authentic expertise with strategic publishing practices**. A well-positioned business guide, a deeply personal memoir, or a spiritually resonant devotional can not only achieve sales success but also generate an enduring platform—something Amazon's algorithm is well-equipped to amplify.

Conclusion

The dominance of non-fiction in the Kindle marketplace is a testament to the evolving demands of digital readers. As more individuals turn to e-books for **education, empowerment, and existential meaning**, Amazon's KDP platform has become a conduit for knowledge distribution at scale.

The categories of **Self-Help**, **Business**, **Biographies**, and **Spirituality** are not just selling well—they are **redefining what success looks like in independent publishing**. For authors equipped with both insight and intent, these genres offer not just a niche, but a formidable domain of influence.

3

Algorithmic Tides

Capitalizing on Trending Subgenres in the KDP Marketplace

Amazon's Kindle Direct Publishing (KDP) ecosystem does not privilege content based on genre, theme, or literary quality. Instead, it is inherently **responsive to consumer demand**, dynamically adjusting exposure based on the market's current appetite. Within this framework, **trending subgenres**—narrower thematic or stylistic niches within broader genres—often rise to prominence due to sharp surges in reader interest. These surges are algorithmically significant: they trigger increased search volume, higher click-through rates, and spikes in conversion, all of which are signals that **propel a book to greater visibility** within Amazon's recommendation architecture.

The Dynamics of Subgenre Discovery

The KDP algorithm is designed to respond to patterns of consumer behavior. It does not possess intrinsic genre preferences; rather, it mirrors reader interests. When large numbers of users begin searching for specific tropes or subgenres, Amazon's systems detect this movement through real-time keyword analytics and purchase histories. Titles that **align with these emerging interests** are then more likely to be recommended—appearing in search suggestions, "Customers Also Bought" lists, email newsletters, and category bestseller charts. As a result, books that are structurally optimized to intersect with a trending niche benefit from **algorithmic magnification**.

This phenomenon has been particularly evident in genre fiction, where subgenres often form around **tropes with strong emotional or cultural resonance**. Consider the ongoing popularity of "**hockey romance**," "**mafia romance**," or "**curvy heroine**" **tropes** in the contemporary romance sector. These subgenres are not random fads but recurring preferences shaped by community discussions, social media trends (especially BookTok), and shifting cultural narratives. As these subgenres gain momentum, **reader search behavior coalesces** around their associated keywords—often with thousands of readers actively looking for new entries that fulfill the trope-specific emotional payoff. For a KDP author, aligning a new release with such subgenres increases the probability that Amazon's algorithm will surface the book to a relevant, eager audience.

Tropes as Discovery Engines

Subgenres function as **discovery vectors** because they allow authors to plug into existing search intent. For example, an author who publishes a mafia romance featuring a morally ambiguous antihero, or a LitRPG novel rooted in game mechanics and progression systems, is not simply creating a narrative—they are **satisfying an established reader expectation**. The algorithm detects that books with these thematic tags are being frequently clicked and purchased, and thus begins to prioritize similar titles across the recommendation engine.

Amazon's internal indexing system is also highly responsive to metadata and content signals. When authors deliberately structure their book titles, subtitles, descriptions, and keyword slots around trending subgenre terms—such as "academy fantasy," "alien romance," or "shifter paranormal"—they increase their odds of appearing in the exact query streams readers are generating. This is particularly true in romance and fantasy, where readers often input highly specific searches (e.g., "grumpy sunshine small-town romance" or "reverse harem academy magic"). Books that **accurately reflect these tropes in their metadata** are more likely to be matched to consumer interest, which in turn catalyzes click-through and conversion, reinforcing the book's ranking in Amazon's proprietary recommendation loops.

Science Fiction, Fantasy, and the Niche Explosion

In the science fiction and fantasy sectors, subgenres like **LitRPG** (literary role-playing game fiction), **progression fantasy**, and **alien romance** have emerged as dominant forces, particularly among digital-first readers. These subgenres thrive on serialized storytelling and gamified mechanics, with strong parallels to fan communities and online gaming culture. The popularity of these niches is measurable in keyword search volume and has been extensively tracked by analytics platforms such as Kindlepreneur.

These subgenres are algorithmically potent for several reasons:

- They attract **highly engaged, repeat readers** who consume multiple titles within a theme.
- They lend themselves to **series development**, increasing lifetime value per customer.
- They generate **community buzz**, often amplified by niche reviewers, Reddit forums, or BookTube influencers.

As such, books that match these emerging preferences and are launched with optimized keywords and on-brand covers benefit from **amplified discoverability**, even with minimal advertising spend.

The Strategic Imperative of Market Alignment

For authors navigating the highly competitive KDP environment, the implication is clear: **alignment with a thriving subgenre dramatically improves a book's commercial trajectory**. This alignment does not mean sacrificing originality or craft. Rather, it entails framing one's work in such a way that it meets **reader expectations already proven to convert**. As self-publishing experts have observed, books that fit neatly within trending subgenres "have a better chance at selling books" simply because they are *easier to match with active demand.*

In practical terms, this involves:

- Conducting regular keyword research to identify rising search phrases.
- Analyzing the bestseller lists in your genre to discern repeated tropes and themes.
- Structuring book titles, descriptions, and metadata around **tropes currently resonating** with readers.
- Choosing covers and branding that visually signal genre and subgenre alignment.
- Rapidly iterating content strategies in response to observable trends in reader behavior.

The Feedback Loop of Popularity

The process is inherently recursive. Once a book begins to gain traction within a trending subgenre, Amazon's algorithm intensifies its exposure—recommending it more widely, ranking it higher in search, and integrating it into "frequently bought together" carousels. This increased visibility results in more sales, which further enhances its algorithmic priority. In this sense, **trending subgenres act as accelerants**, offering the algorithm a clearer path to surface and reward high-converting content.

Conclusion

In the Amazon KDP ecosystem, trending subgenres are not ephemeral distractions; they are **powerful levers** for discoverability and profitability. The algorithm may not favor specific genres a priori, but it *does* consistently reward books that tap into documented reader preferences. For authors aiming to maximize visibility, tapping into an emerging subgenre or popular trope is not merely a stylistic choice—it is a strategic imperative. By aligning narrative design with identifiable market demand, authors dramatically increase their likelihood of being lifted by Amazon's algorithmic currents— *and reaching the readers already waiting for stories just like theirs.*

4

The Power of Clustering

How Genre-Based Recommendation Loops Drive Visibility on Amazon KDP

Amazon's vast e-commerce infrastructure is powered by complex algorithms, but none are more commercially consequential for authors than its **recommendation systems**. Among these, features like "Customers Also Bought," "Recommended for You," and personalized promotional emails form an interconnected matrix that amplifies visibility for books through **genre clustering**. This phenomenon—where books are recommended based on proximity to other books within the same genre—has a profound impact on discoverability, sales momentum, and the long-term viability of an author's catalogue.

The Mechanics of Genre Clustering

At its core, genre clustering is a function of Amazon's **collaborative filtering algorithm**—a statistical technique that recommends products based on patterns in user behavior. When multiple customers purchase or engage with the same book, Amazon's system identifies shared preferences and uses them to **build associative networks**. If a large number of readers who bought Book A also bought Book B, Book B will begin to appear in the "Customers Also Bought" section of Book A's product page. The system does not interpret thematic similarity directly; rather, it **infers it from consumer behavior**, which frequently aligns with genre.

In practical terms, this means that if a reader purchases a best-selling cozy mystery, Amazon is algorithmically primed to recommend other cozy mysteries—not just based on metadata or subgenre tags, but based on observed **co-purchase behavior**. These patterns become self-reinforcing: the more readers buy similar books, the tighter the genre cluster becomes, and the more those books are promoted together.

Implications for Genre Fiction Authors

This behavior is especially beneficial for **authors writing within clearly defined genres**, such as romance, thrillers, or fantasy. These genres have well-established conventions and highly engaged readerships, which increases the likelihood of pattern recognition by Amazon's systems. A romance author, for instance, who releases a second book in a popular series will often see their new title appear in the "Also Bought" lists of the previous books. This **internal cross-promotion** is a powerful advantage, allowing the author to build a self-sustaining marketing engine based on past reader behavior.

The clustering effect also enhances the performance of books written in **episodic or serialized formats**. For example, detective series or romance sagas with recurring characters or interconnected plots benefit from this algorithmic tendency. When readers consume Book One and then immediately purchase Book Two, the system learns to associate these books— and, by extension, the entire series—with one another. This clustering triggers not only sidebar recommendations but also **email promotions**, wherein Amazon notifies readers that a new release from a previously purchased series or author is now available.

The Role of Audience Mapping and Genre Precision

To benefit from genre clustering, an author must ensure that their book is easily identifiable within its genre. This involves aligning **cover design, title conventions, metadata (especially categories and keywords), and blurb content** with the expectations of the target audience. The clearer the genre signal, the more accurately Amazon can position the book within its ecosystem of related titles.

When this alignment is successful, the algorithm can **map your book onto a specific reader segment**, increasing the probability that it will appear in genre-specific recommendations. If your book does not clearly fit into a defined genre category—or worse, blends incompatible tropes without sufficient clarity—it may fail to cluster effectively. This leads to a weaker presence in the "Also Bought" and "Recommended" feeds, effectively isolating the book from its natural audience and reducing its discoverability.

Reinforcement Through Personalized Promotion

Beyond product page placements, Amazon uses genre clustering to power **personalized email campaigns**. These emails are triggered by user behavior and reflect patterns identified in the larger purchasing ecosystem. If a customer buys a book that frequently appears in your title's "Also Bought" list, Amazon may recommend your book to that customer—even if they have never heard of you. This latent promotional mechanism is especially potent for midlist or emerging authors whose work becomes associated with more popular titles in the same genre.

Moreover, these algorithmic promotions can have a **compounding effect**. A surge in visibility due to inclusion in an email campaign or "Also Bought" carousel may lead to a spike in sales, which in turn further strengthens the clustering relationship. The book is then promoted to an even broader pool of readers, creating a **positive feedback loop** of increasing exposure and sales—a dynamic sometimes referred to as the "Amazon flywheel."

Strategic Considerations for KDP Authors

Given the structural logic of Amazon's recommendation systems, authors can take several concrete steps to maximize the benefits of genre clustering:

- **Write in a well-defined genre**, and signal this clearly through cover design and metadata.
- **Publish in series**, or at minimum, thematically linked works that can be clustered through reader behavior.
- **Encourage sequenced purchasing** by using back matter links, preview chapters, or pricing incentives to guide readers from one title to the next.
- **Leverage promotions strategically**, particularly around launch periods, to spike sales velocity and initiate clustering associations.
- **Collaborate with genre-adjacent authors**, for example through newsletter swaps or boxed sets, to seed co-purchase patterns that the algorithm may pick up on.

These strategies are not simply marketing techniques—they are methods of engaging with Amazon's underlying algorithm in a way that increases the likelihood of sustained discoverability.

Conclusion

Genre clustering is not a passive byproduct of Amazon's platform—it is a **core mechanism of content discovery**. By organizing books into behaviorally defined genre clusters, Amazon ensures that each reader is continuously presented with options they are most likely to enjoy. For KDP authors, understanding and leveraging this system is crucial. A book that fits snugly into its genre cluster has a significantly higher chance of being surfaced, purchased, and retained in Amazon's algorithmic memory. In an ecosystem driven by data and reader behavior, **genre precision and strategic clustering are not optional—they are essential for long-term**

success.

II

Format Preferences and Format-Based Promotion Patterns

"Format Preferences and Format-Based Promotion Patterns"
examines how Amazon's KDP algorithm treats different
publishing formats—eBooks, print, and audiobooks—based on
*reader behavior and platform priorities. "**Digital Dominance**"*
reflects the primacy of Kindle eBooks, which drive most sales and
enjoy algorithmic advantages like real-time ranking and KU
*exposure. "**The Strategic Value of Print**" highlights how*
paperbacks excel in niches like non-fiction and children's books,
*earning separate bestseller rankings. "**Exclusivity for Exposure**"*
explores how enrolling in KDP Select (Kindle Unlimited
exclusivity) can unlock algorithm-driven promotion.
*"**Format-Specific Promotion**" covers tools like Kindle*
Countdown Deals, which only apply to digital formats. Finally,
*"**Multi-Format Synergy**" emphasizes how offering your book in*
eBook, print, and audiobook formats enhances discoverability and
credibility across Amazon's marketplace.

5

Digital Dominance

Kindle E-Books and the Algorithmic Advantage in the KDP Marketplace

In the landscape of Amazon Kindle Direct Publishing (KDP), the digital format reigns supreme. While the platform offers authors the ability to publish in multiple formats—including paperback and hardcover—**Kindle e-books overwhelmingly drive visibility, rankings, and sales**, particularly for independent authors. This supremacy is not merely a matter of reader preference; it is structurally embedded in the design of Amazon's algorithmic infrastructure. For authors seeking to maximize their reach and revenue, understanding the centrality of the e-book format is essential.

E-Books as the Sales Engine

The consumption habits of Amazon readers reveal a clear bias toward digital. For most indie authors, Kindle e-books—especially when enrolled in **Kindle Unlimited (KU)**—generate the vast majority of total sales. A common revenue split reported among successful self-publishers is **85% digital to 15% print**, with digital further divided between **paid Kindle downloads and KU page reads**. In one documented case, the breakdown consisted of approximately 30% direct e-book purchases and 55% Kindle Unlimited consumption, leaving only 15% for all print formats combined (Holmes, 2023).

These figures reflect a broader truth: **digital reading is the engine of discoverability and scalability** on Amazon. Readers gravitate to the convenience, affordability, and immediacy of e-books, especially in genre fiction. As a result, Amazon's own systems are built to privilege e-book sales as the primary indicator of reader interest.

The Algorithmic Weight of Kindle Performance

The Kindle Store operates as a semi-autonomous ecosystem within Amazon, complete with its own **best-seller rankings, promotional opportunities, and recommendation loops**. The **Kindle Best Seller Rank (KBSR)** is updated hourly and is highly responsive to recent sales velocity. This agility allows for rapid ascents when a title gains momentum—whether through organic discovery, advertising, or promotional pricing. Once a Kindle title climbs the KBSR, it becomes eligible for greater visibility through:

- Inclusion in the **Kindle best-seller lists** by genre and subgenre,
- Feature placement in the **"Hot New Releases"** section (within the first 30 days of publication),
- Increased exposure in **"Customers Also Bought"** and "Recommended for You" carousels.

In contrast, paperback and hardcover editions are **subject to slower, less dynamic ranking systems**. While the Books Store (print division) also maintains best-seller charts, these are not updated with the same frequency or algorithmic intensity as their Kindle counterparts. Moreover, there are fewer promotional tools available for print books, making it more difficult for them to achieve breakout visibility without external support.

Kindle Unlimited: The Subscription Multiplier

The inclusion of a book in Kindle Unlimited via **KDP Select** introduces a second layer of digital dominance. KU allows readers to "borrow" e-books at no direct cost per title, yet authors are compensated via the **Kindle Edition Normalized Page (KENP) read model**. This system is uniquely aligned with algorithmic ranking: **KU page reads count toward sales velocity**, thereby boosting a book's best-seller rank as though it were purchased outright.

This dynamic creates a compounding advantage for e-book authors who enroll in KU:

- High page reads generate royalties,
- Those reads count toward sales momentum,
- Sales momentum increases visibility,
- Increased visibility leads to more reads.

For indie authors, particularly in high-consumption genres like romance, fantasy, and thriller, KU participation often proves critical for reaching the **top tiers of Kindle visibility**. The platform's emphasis on reader engagement—measured in pages read rather than books sold—also incentivizes authors to focus on pacing, story hooks, and series development, all of which improve retention and monetization in the KU model.

Print's Limited Role in the Visibility Economy

While print formats (especially paperbacks) remain relevant for certain categories—such as children's books, cookbooks, and academic titles—their role in Amazon's **algorithmic economy is secondary**. Print books lack access to many of the promotional tools available to Kindle editions. For instance:

- Print books cannot participate in **Kindle Countdown Deals** or **Free

Book Promotions.

- They are not included in **Kindle-specific bestseller lists**, which are often more trafficked.
- Page reads via Kindle Unlimited do not apply, as the program is exclusive to digital content.

Moreover, the physical constraints of print—such as higher production costs, longer shipping times, and limited international availability—reduce the frictionless scalability that defines the Kindle platform. These structural limitations make print a valuable **supplement** to an author's catalogue, but rarely a **growth catalyst**.

Strategic Implications for Authors

For authors publishing through KDP, the dominance of Kindle e-books presents clear strategic directives:

- Prioritize Kindle edition optimization through metadata, pricing, and promotional alignment.
- Enroll titles in KDP Select to tap into the KU reader base, especially for fiction.
- Use the e-book format to generate momentum, then offer paperback and hardcover as ancillary formats for reader preference and expanded reach.
- Track Kindle Best Seller Rank as the primary indicator of visibility and algorithmic favorability.

While print can serve important branding, gifting, and legacy functions, it is the e-book that moves the algorithm. A paperback may grace a shelf, but it is the Kindle edition that **triggers the engine of discovery** on Amazon's digital shelves.

Conclusion

In the KDP publishing ecosystem, format is not neutral. Amazon's algorithms place disproportionate emphasis on **Kindle e-book performance**, and for good reason: it is the format that best aligns with consumer behavior, platform scalability, and real-time responsiveness. For authors seeking to succeed on Amazon—not just in terms of sales, but in terms of sustained algorithmic promotion—the **Kindle edition is the format that matters most**. Digital dominance is not a passing trend; it is the structural reality of the world's largest self-publishing platform.

6

The Strategic Value of Print

Paperbacks and Niche Market Visibility on Amazon KDP

While the Kindle ecosystem dominates much of the visibility and revenue within Amazon's Kindle Direct Publishing (KDP) platform, the **print market—specifically paperbacks and hardcovers—retains a strategic role**, especially within certain genres and consumer demographics. Though often secondary to e-books in terms of volume, print books can command meaningful algorithmic attention when targeted effectively and positioned within the right market niches.

Distinct Ecosystems: Print vs. Kindle Rankings

One of the most critical structural elements authors must understand is that **Amazon's print and Kindle stores operate on separate ranking systems**. The Kindle Best Seller Rank (KBSR) is distinct from the Best Seller Rank in the Books store (which includes both paperbacks and hardcovers). This distinction allows a title to perform modestly in its Kindle edition while simultaneously achieving **category bestseller status in print**, particularly within niche or low-competition categories.

For example, a non-fiction title might rank outside the top 5,000 in Kindle but sit comfortably within the top 100—or even top 10—in a narrow paperback subcategory such as *Health & Wellness > Grief & Bereavement* or *Cooking > Mediterranean Diet*. This **parallel visibility path** gives authors an alternate route to recognition, especially in genres where physical format is functionally or emotionally preferred by the reader base.

Genre-Specific Demand for Physical Books

Certain genres naturally skew toward print purchases. These include:

- **Non-Fiction Reference**: Readers often prefer tangible copies of cookbooks, self-help guides, academic texts, and planners. The tactile and navigational advantages of print are indispensable in these categories. A printed cookbook, for instance, is easier to use in a kitchen setting than a tablet or e-reader.
- **Children's Literature**: Physical books dominate the children's market due to the **visual, developmental, and parent-child interaction factors** involved in reading. Picture books, early readers, and activity books are rarely consumed digitally. KDP authors targeting this demographic must prioritize **high-quality paperback (or hardcover) editions** optimized for full-color interior layouts and durable binding.
- **Workbooks and Educational Materials**: In educational publishing, physical formats often retain priority due to annotation needs, classroom use, and regulatory compatibility (e.g., institutions requiring ISBN-linked print editions).

In these genres, **readers not only prefer print—they expect it**. As a result, paperback and hardcover sales can constitute a disproportionately large share of revenue, and the Books store algorithm reflects this behavior by prioritizing well-performing print titles in relevant listings.

Algorithmic Visibility in the Books Store

When a paperback begins to sell consistently, Amazon's algorithmic systems start to surface it through various promotional placements in the Books store. These include:

- **Category bestseller lists** specific to paperback/hardcover formats.
- **"Frequently Bought Together"** pairings that link a Kindle edition with its print counterpart.
- Inclusion in **home page carousels**, personalized book emails, and related-title recommendations within the Books store.

It is important to note that a well-performing paperback edition can **lift the visibility of the corresponding Kindle version**, especially when buyers are shown both formats side by side. This cross-format synergy can improve a book's overall performance, helping it reach a broader range of consumer preferences. Moreover, print sales generate reviews and increase the book's aggregate star rating, which in turn improves both Kindle and paperback conversion rates.

Print as a Niche Visibility Strategy

While e-books dominate general fiction markets due to their instant accessibility and low cost, **print formats offer a niche-specific visibility strategy**. For authors operating in saturated digital genres, strategically targeting print-dominant niches may provide a more accessible path to sales traction. For instance, entering a tightly focused non-fiction category with a well-packaged paperback may yield more immediate chart visibility than attempting to climb high-competition Kindle fiction lists.

Moreover, authors can take advantage of **multi-format publishing** to enhance discoverability:

- Offering both print and Kindle editions increases a title's footprint on

Amazon.

- The presence of a print edition can **boost credibility**, especially in non-fiction genres where readers associate physical format with professionalism and reliability.
- In certain cases, a paperback priced higher than its Kindle counterpart can generate **higher profit margins**, especially if paired with direct sales strategies or bulk purchasing channels (e.g., speaking engagements, school orders, or corporate training).

Constraints and Considerations

Despite its value, print carries inherent limitations:

- **Longer production and shipping times** reduce impulse buy potential.
- **Higher manufacturing costs** require careful pricing strategy to maintain margins.
- Print editions are not eligible for certain Kindle-exclusive promotional tools (e.g., Free Book Promotions, Countdown Deals).
- International distribution of print books may incur logistical challenges, particularly for color interiors or non-standard trim sizes.

As such, print should be approached as a **complementary component of a broader publishing strategy**, rather than a primary growth engine—unless the genre or audience specifically demands it.

Conclusion

In Amazon's KDP platform, **print books matter most where the reader's experience demands physicality**—in tactile, visual, or reference-driven genres. Though e-books remain the algorithmic focal point due to their scale and responsiveness, print editions serve a vital role in niche market engagement, credibility building, and cross-format promotion. For authors operating in non-fiction, children's, and reference categories, the paperback is more than a legacy format; it is a strategic asset capable of unlocking unique visibility within Amazon's Books ecosystem.

7

Exclusivity for Exposure

KDP Select, Kindle Unlimited, and the Algorithmic Edge

In Amazon's Kindle Direct Publishing (KDP) ecosystem, **format is not merely a question of file type**—it is also a strategic decision with far-reaching implications for visibility, revenue, and platform reach. One of the most consequential format-related choices authors face is whether to enroll their e-book in **KDP Select**, a program that grants access to **Kindle Unlimited (KU)** in exchange for **90-day exclusivity** to the Amazon platform. This decision directly impacts how the Amazon algorithm ranks and promotes a book, especially for genre fiction authors seeking traction in an increasingly competitive marketplace.

What is KDP Select?

KDP Select is a voluntary opt-in program for Kindle e-books. By enrolling, the author agrees to **digital exclusivity**—the e-book cannot be distributed through any other retailer or platform for the duration of the 90-day term. In exchange, Amazon offers several benefits:

1. **Inclusion in Kindle Unlimited**, Amazon's subscription service for readers.
2. **Eligibility for promotional tools**, such as Kindle Countdown Deals and Free Book Promotions.
3. **Algorithmic preference and additional discoverability**, especially within KU-dedicated recommendation spaces.

The **trade-off** is clear: broader reach within Amazon versus wider distribution across platforms like Apple Books, Kobo, Barnes & Noble, and others. However, for many authors—particularly in high-consumption genres like romance, thriller, and fantasy—the algorithmic rewards of exclusivity often **outweigh the cost of limited availability**.

Kindle Unlimited and Algorithmic Visibility

The core advantage of KDP Select lies in the visibility provided by **Kindle Unlimited**. KU is a subscription model where readers pay a monthly fee to access an unlimited number of participating e-books. Authors are compensated not by unit sale, but by **pages read**—measured in Kindle Edition Normalized Pages (KENP). Importantly, **KU borrows and reads count toward Amazon's bestseller ranking system**, just like direct purchases.

This structural feature of KU makes it an **algorithmic equalizer**—an e-book that is read deeply by KU users can rise rapidly through the **Kindle Best Seller Rank (KBSR)**, even if relatively few units are purchased outright. As Reedsy explains, KDP Select gives access to **"all-important Kindle Unlimited readers whose borrows will also help push you further up the list"** (Reedsy, 2024). For books in KU, **volume of page reads translates directly into both income and algorithmic attention**.

How KU Boosts Discoverability

Kindle Unlimited does not merely offer access to a new pool of readers; it is also a **promotional ecosystem in itself**, with numerous pathways to visibility:

- **"Free with Kindle Unlimited" badges** on product pages, which attract KU subscribers.
- **Dedicated KU categories**, such as "Top 100 in Kindle Unlimited," where readers browse exclusively within the subscription environment.
- **Increased presence in "Customers Also Bought" and "Recommended for You" feeds**, especially for KU-heavy customers.
- **Amazon-generated emails and homepage carousels** targeted at KU readers based on their borrowing habits.

Amazon actively promotes KU content because it enhances the value of the KU subscription model. Therefore, books enrolled in KDP Select are more likely to be **algorithmically favored in customer-facing interfaces**, as they contribute to Amazon's retention and revenue strategy. The practical result: **higher rankings, more impressions, and increased organic traffic** for titles inside the KU system.

The Strategic Case for Exclusivity

Choosing KDP Select is particularly advantageous for authors in genres with **high reader volume and strong serial consumption patterns**. Many KU subscribers are voracious genre readers, and they often prioritize books that are:

- Part of a series,
- Aligned with familiar tropes or subgenres,
- Available at no additional cost under their subscription.

This makes KDP Select ideal for authors who publish **frequently, write in series, or target niche genre audiences**—all behaviors that encourage binge reading, high KENP counts, and strong algorithmic performance.

Additionally, KDP Select's promotional tools (such as **Kindle Countdown Deals** and **Free Promotions**) provide crucial levers for launch and relaunch strategies. While these tools are unavailable to non-enrolled titles, they can **artificially spike sales or borrows**, which the algorithm reads as a surge in popularity, further boosting exposure.

Limitations and Considerations

The exclusivity requirement remains the most significant constraint of KDP Select. Authors lose the ability to reach readers on:

- Apple Books,
- Google Play,
- Kobo,
- Nook (Barnes & Noble),
- Independent platforms and library networks.

This trade-off may be untenable for authors with an established reader base outside Amazon or those prioritizing wide distribution and ownership over subscription-based access. Furthermore, KU's **per-page royalty model** may result in lower earnings for books with shorter lengths or lower read-through rates, particularly in non-fiction genres where readers tend to sample selectively rather than read cover to cover.

Thus, while KDP Select enhances visibility within Amazon, it does so at the expense of **platform independence and market diversification**. Authors must weigh short-term algorithmic acceleration against long-term strategic flexibility.

Conclusion

In Amazon's publishing ecosystem, **KDP Select is a powerful mechanism for increasing visibility, rankings, and reader engagement**, particularly within the Kindle Unlimited network. By funneling a book into Amazon's algorithmic core—where KU readers, page-read metrics, and exclusive promotions all converge—KDP Select offers indie authors a pathway to accelerated discoverability. For those writing in KU-heavy genres and willing to forgo broad distribution, **the exclusivity of KDP Select is not a limitation—it is a gateway to greater algorithmic leverage and sustained digital presence**.

8

Format-Specific Promotion

Leveraging Kindle E-Book Tools for Algorithmic Momentum

In Amazon's Kindle Direct Publishing (KDP) ecosystem, promotional capability is not evenly distributed across formats. The platform provides a **robust suite of promotional tools exclusively for Kindle e-books**, particularly those enrolled in KDP Select, while **print formats—paperbacks and hardcovers—remain comparatively static** in their marketing potential. This asymmetry has profound implications for an author's launch strategy, sales momentum, and long-term visibility, especially when attempting to influence Amazon's recommendation algorithms.

The Advantage of Digital Promotions

Kindle e-books enrolled in KDP Select are uniquely positioned to benefit from two high-impact promotional options:

1. **Free Promotions**: Authors can set their e-book to be free for up to five days within each 90-day Select enrollment period.
2. **Kindle Countdown Deals**: These allow authors to offer time-limited

price reductions while retaining a 70% royalty rate, provided the book is priced between $2.99 and $9.99.

These tools serve as **algorithmic triggers**, driving short-term visibility spikes that can generate long-term benefits. For instance, a free promotion may not contribute to a title's **paid Best Seller Rank (BSR)**, but it can propel the book to the top of the **"Top Free" charts**, where thousands of readers may discover and download it. These downloads, while not monetized directly, can lead to:

- **Increased exposure in search results and genre pages**,
- **More reviews**, which improve conversion rates and social proof,
- **Downstream purchases** of sequels or related titles,
- **Improved internal ranking** via Amazon's **popularity metrics**, which factor heavily into recommendation engines.

According to Reedsy, free promotions influence Amazon's **internal ranking systems in a quantity-over-quality fashion**, rewarding books that move large volumes, even at a $0 price point. The key insight is that **activity—measured in clicks, downloads, and reader engagement—is the signal Amazon uses to determine relevance**, regardless of direct revenue during the promotion window.

Countdown Deals and Sales Velocity

Kindle Countdown Deals provide a **hybrid benefit** of discount pricing and royalty protection. Because the sale price appears with a timer and strikethrough (e.g., "$0.99 – ends in 2 days"), this type of promotion creates a sense of urgency, improving **click-through rate (CTR)** and conversion. A successful Countdown Deal that results in a sharp uptick in purchases can **catapult a book up the paid BSR rankings**, which in turn places the book in "Hot New Releases," "Best Sellers in [Genre]," and other algorithmically influential positions.

These visibility enhancements generate **compound discoverability**: the more customers engage with the promoted e-book, the more Amazon's algorithm surfaces it to other readers with similar preferences.

Paperbacks and Promotional Constraints

In stark contrast to Kindle e-books, **paperbacks lack access to Amazon-run promotional programs**. Authors cannot make a paperback free or run a timed discount managed by the platform. While one can manually change a paperback's price, there is no built-in infrastructure to support countdown-style urgency or free listing in a curated storefront. This limits paperbacks in several key ways:

- **They cannot compete for placement on promotional charts**, such as "Top Free" or "Limited-Time Deals."
- **They do not benefit from real-time visibility surges** triggered by Amazon-supported price manipulations.
- **They do not have promotional visibility sections dedicated to discounted or featured titles.**

As a result, **paperbacks must rely solely on organic search, customer demand, and cross-format linkage to gain algorithmic traction**.

Strategic Implications: Lead with Digital, Upsell to Print

Given the promotional disparity between formats, a common best practice among successful KDP authors is to **launch the Kindle edition with an aggressive promotional strategy**, using either free days or Countdown Deals to build immediate momentum. Once the e-book establishes algorithmic visibility—appearing in "Also Bought" recommendations, ranking in relevant subcategories, and accumulating reviews—authors can then **upsell readers to higher-margin print formats**.

This model offers several strategic advantages:

- **E-book readers may purchase the paperback version** after enjoying the digital edition (especially in gifting contexts).
- **Visibility gains from the e-book version benefit the paperback indirectly**, due to Amazon's practice of displaying linked editions together on a single product page.
- **The perceived value of the paperback is increased**, particularly if it is priced higher and positioned as a premium reading or display experience.

In effect, the Kindle edition acts as a **loss leader or momentum builder**, generating visibility and engagement that the algorithm recognizes, while the paperback reaps the rewards of that attention at full price.

Conclusion

Amazon's promotional infrastructure is **designed around Kindle e-books**, particularly those in the KDP Select program. Free Promotions and Countdown Deals offer powerful mechanisms to generate **sales velocity, reader engagement, and algorithmic visibility**, all of which are critical to success in a crowded digital marketplace. In contrast, print formats offer limited promotional functionality, and their visibility depends largely on organic interest or the spillover from a strong digital campaign. For authors aiming to maximize discoverability and reader reach, **leveraging e-book promotions as the spearhead of a broader publishing strategy remains essential**—with paperbacks serving as an ancillary product that benefits from the digital title's success.

9

Multi-Format Synergy

Leveraging Audiobooks and Format Diversity to Amplify Amazon Visibility

In the digital publishing ecosystem, where discoverability and conversion are heavily mediated by algorithmic ranking and customer behavior, format diversification has emerged as a strategic imperative. While **Kindle Direct Publishing (KDP)** is the primary platform for independent authors, extending a book into **multiple formats—especially by adding an audiobook via Audible/ACX—offers tangible benefits** for visibility, credibility, and cross-format sales on Amazon. Even though audiobooks are not technically part of KDP, they interact with Amazon's marketplace and algorithms in a manner that can significantly **amplify a title's presence and performance**.

Audiobooks and the Amazon Ecosystem

Audiobooks have become a dominant force in consumer reading habits, with the market for spoken-word content growing rapidly across global territories. For self-published authors, Amazon provides access to the audiobook market through **Audible and ACX (Audiobook Creation Exchange)**. These platforms allow authors to produce audiobooks either by self-narration or by hiring professional narrators on a royalty-share or flat-rate basis.

Once published, the audiobook is listed on **Audible, Amazon, and iTunes**, and, crucially, **Amazon links the audiobook to the corresponding Kindle and paperback editions** via the product page. This cross-linking creates a **unified retail presence**, presenting the book as a cohesive, multi-format product that enhances buyer confidence and improves conversion.

Cross-Promotion and the "Complete Product" Signal

When a book is available in Kindle, print, and audiobook formats, Amazon **displays all versions on the same product detail page**, allowing customers to toggle between formats. This triad of availability **signals professionalism and completeness**, characteristics that are algorithmically and behaviorally favorable. Readers and listeners alike are more likely to trust and purchase a book that offers multiple options—especially in categories where buyers may switch between formats depending on context (e.g., listening during a commute, then continuing the story in e-book form).

Furthermore, Amazon sometimes **cross-promotes the audiobook edition directly** through a "**Add Audible narration**" option on the Kindle book's product page. This promotes **Whispersync for Voice**, a feature that synchronizes audiobook and e-book progress across devices. Whispersync not only enhances user convenience but also **increases customer engagement time within Amazon's ecosystem**—a signal that Amazon values highly when prioritizing content in recommendations and visibility algorithms.

Algorithmic Impact of Multi-Format Availability

While the core KDP algorithm is primarily influenced by Kindle e-book performance, a book's overall **sales volume, customer engagement, and conversion rate across all formats** feeds into broader Amazon marketplace metrics. Notably:

- **Strong audiobook sales contribute to the book's rank in the overall "Books" category**, boosting discoverability outside the Kindle-only environment.
- **Audiobook reviews**, even though hosted separately on Audible, enhance the perceived authority and quality of the title when displayed on Amazon's product pages.
- **Multi-format listings improve conversion rates**—a key metric used by Amazon's A9 search algorithm to determine product relevance and ranking.
- The presence of an audiobook often leads to **bundled purchases**, where customers buy both the Kindle and Audible editions, thus increasing overall revenue and sales signals.

Together, these factors create a **synergistic feedback loop**: the availability of an audiobook strengthens the product's appeal, boosts visibility through sales and engagement, and thus leads to more exposure across Amazon's algorithmically curated storefronts.

Strategic Use Cases for Audiobook Integration

Adding an audiobook is particularly advantageous in the following scenarios:

- **Non-fiction categories**, where readers often seek flexibility in how they consume content (e.g., business, self-help, personal development).
- **Long-form fiction series**, where audio binge-listening mirrors the behavior of e-book series readers in Kindle Unlimited.

- **Memoirs and narrative nonfiction**, which benefit from author-narrated versions that offer authenticity and emotional resonance.

For authors targeting premium markets or seeking to build long-term brand equity, audiobook production also enhances **perceived authorial authority**. Readers associate the presence of multiple formats with serious authorship and a commitment to quality—traits that influence both customer trust and long-term discoverability.

Limitations and Considerations

Despite its advantages, audiobook production entails logistical and financial investment. The author must:

- Choose between **royalty-share agreements or upfront production fees**,
- Ensure **high production standards**, as audio listeners are less forgiving of poor narration or sound quality,
- Prepare a manuscript suitable for narration, which may involve revising visuals, charts, or references that don't translate well to audio.

Moreover, while audio sales can support visibility, the **primary algorithmic drivers within KDP remain e-book sales and Kindle Unlimited page reads**. Therefore, the audiobook should be viewed not as a substitute for a strong Kindle launch, but as a **strategic extension of a successful publication model**.

Conclusion

In Amazon's algorithm-driven marketplace, **a book's success is increasingly influenced by its breadth of format availability**. While the Kindle e-book is the foundation of discoverability and sales within KDP, the addition of an audiobook via Audible/ACX can significantly amplify a title's reach, appeal, and algorithmic positioning. By presenting a unified, multi-format presence, authors can enhance their credibility, engage more customers, and ultimately increase their chances of sustained commercial success. In an environment where every reader touchpoint matters, **format diversification is no longer optional—it is an essential component of modern independent publishing strategy**.

III

Writing Style and Story Structure that Engage the Algorithm

"Writing Style and Story Structure that Engage the Algorithm" delves into how reader behavior—not literary merit—drives Amazon's promotional logic. "Engagement Over Elegance" underscores that the algorithm rewards books that keep readers turning pages, not those with poetic prose. "Hooked from Page One" stresses the importance of compelling openings to boost conversion and retention. "Compounding Visibility" refers to how page reads, reviews, and sequels generate momentum that reinforces your book's discoverability. "Writing to Market" advocates aligning story elements with proven genre expectations to satisfy demand. Finally, "Consistency as Strategy" shows that reliable output in tone, pacing, and series installments strengthens author branding and keeps the algorithm favorably engaged.

10

Engagement Over Elegance

How Amazon's Algorithm Rewards Reader Behavior, Not Literary Merit

In the digital marketplace of Amazon Kindle Direct Publishing (KDP), **reader engagement—not literary quality—is the dominant currency** of success. Contrary to traditional publishing paradigms, where manuscripts are evaluated by editors for artistic merit, Amazon's recommendation algorithms are agnostic to style, theme, or prose sophistication. As industry experts have noted, **"Amazon's algorithm doesn't care how good your book is"** in a literary sense—it **"can't read"** (Coverrater.com). Instead, it evaluates your book **based solely on how readers interact with it**.

This fundamental reality shifts the locus of power from the page to the platform. Success is not determined by the intrinsic quality of writing but by the **observable patterns of reader behavior**: how often a book is downloaded, how long readers engage with it, whether they finish it, and whether they purchase other books by the same author.

Behavioral Metrics: The Algorithm's Lens

Amazon's algorithm is designed to detect and promote books that **stimulate, retain, and satisfy readers**. The key metrics it tracks are:

- **Reading time and completion rate**: Especially for books in **Kindle Unlimited (KU)**, Amazon monitors how many **Kindle Edition Normalized Pages (KENP)** are read. A book that is finished more often sends a stronger signal of reader satisfaction than one that is abandoned early.
- **Purchase-to-read ratio**: The algorithm evaluates what percentage of buyers actually read the book. Low read-through suggests a mismatch between the promise of the cover/blurb and the content itself, which may reduce future exposure.
- **Follow-through behavior**: When readers finish one book and immediately **purchase another book from the same author**, the system flags this as a positive indicator of content satisfaction and author trustworthiness.
- **Review patterns**: While not every reader leaves a review, a consistent stream of favorable, verified reviews—particularly shortly after launch—enhances the algorithm's perception of a book's quality and appeal.

Together, these metrics form an **engagement profile**, which determines whether a book should be promoted in Amazon's internal systems—such as "Customers Also Bought," "Recommended for You," and targeted email campaigns.

The Primacy of Reader Retention in Kindle Unlimited

For titles enrolled in KDP Select and available through Kindle Unlimited, **reader retention is a direct revenue factor**. Authors are paid per page read, not per download. Consequently, books that **keep readers engaged for longer periods generate higher KENP earnings**. More importantly, consistent page reads across a wide user base **boost the title's standing in Amazon's algorithmic rankings**, making it more likely to appear in "Top Titles in KU" and similar promotional slots.

This structure incentivizes authors to **craft narratives that maximize engagement**. Fast pacing, cliffhanger chapter endings, emotionally resonant arcs, and compelling character development are not merely artistic choices—they are tactical decisions that directly affect a book's discoverability and profitability.

As Automateed.com notes, **"writing engaging content that keeps readers hooked certainly helps"** because it leads to deeper reading, repeat engagement, and greater algorithmic favor. The more addictive the reading experience, the more the algorithm takes notice.

The Series Effect: Repeat Engagement as a Growth Engine

One of the clearest demonstrations of engagement-based algorithmic reward is the **performance of book series**. When a reader finishes Book One and immediately buys Book Two, Amazon interprets this as a strong validation of both the book and the author. This behavior:

- Enhances the visibility of the entire series,
- Triggers Amazon's email campaigns to readers who purchased earlier volumes,
- Encourages the algorithm to surface other books in the series in "Also Bought" carousels and genre recommendation feeds.

Series also facilitate **repeat KENP earnings** in KU, as binge readers may consume multiple books back-to-back. This pattern of sustained engagement from the same reader base creates a **compounding visibility effect**, reinforcing the author's presence in the Kindle marketplace.

Implications for Authors: Engagement as Design Principle

Given that the algorithm rewards engagement, authors must **reorient their creative process around the reader's experience**. While artistic integrity remains important, so too does the ability to **hold attention and generate emotional momentum**. Key tactics include:

- **Opening with a strong hook**: Readers browsing the sample are more likely to buy if the first few pages create curiosity or tension.
- **Maintaining narrative propulsion**: Avoid long exposition or unnecessary digressions; each chapter should move the story or argument forward.
- **Ending chapters with forward motion**: Especially in fiction, cliffhangers and unresolved tensions prompt readers to keep turning pages.
- **Optimizing for bingeability**: Shorter chapters, clear structure, and consistent tone help readers stay immersed longer.

It is not necessary to compromise quality in pursuit of engagement. Rather, **literary craftsmanship and reader psychology must operate in tandem**. A beautifully written book that fails to sustain interest will underperform algorithmically; a competently written book that captivates readers will thrive.

Conclusion

Amazon's algorithm does not reward literary brilliance in isolation. It rewards books that **perform**—books that are read, finished, reviewed, and followed up with further purchases. In this data-driven environment, **engagement is the true marker of value**. Authors who understand this— and design their books accordingly—position themselves for algorithmic amplification and long-term success. The lesson is clear: to rise on Amazon, it is not enough to write well. One must write **compellingly enough to hold readers hostage**, because **every page turned is a signal to the machine** that your book deserves to be seen.

11

Hooked from Page One

The Algorithmic Value of Strong Openings and Tight Pacing in KDP Success

In the Kindle Direct Publishing (KDP) marketplace, where visibility is algorithmically determined and reader attention spans are short, the opening pages of a book are not merely artistic—they are strategic. **A compelling hook and sustained narrative momentum are essential not only for reader satisfaction but for algorithmic survival.** Amazon's systems track user behavior from the moment a shopper lands on a product page to the final page read, and they reward books that consistently provoke and sustain reader engagement. Thus, successful KDP authors must prioritize **fast-paced, hook-heavy storytelling** as a matter of algorithmic necessity.

The Importance of the First Few Pages

The most decisive moment in a book's life cycle is often **the sample read**—the free preview offered to browsers before purchase. This window, typically encompassing the first 10% of the book, is Amazon's version of the audition stage. If the reader is not immediately intrigued, they will click away. If they are, the algorithm notes a **high conversion rate**: the number of people who buy the book after sampling it.

This conversion rate is critical. A book that consistently turns browsers into buyers is deemed "relevant" and "high-performing" by Amazon's recommendation engine. As Book Boss Academy notes, **"a compelling opening chapter or prologue that immediately grabs attention can convert a browser into a buyer,"** and this conversion directly feeds the system that decides whether to boost a book through "Customers Also Bought," "Recommended for You," and genre-specific email campaigns.

In short, the strength of the opening pages does not just affect a single purchase—it determines **whether Amazon's algorithm will support or ignore your book.**

Pacing as a Retention Tool

After the sale or download, the next algorithmically significant variable is **reader engagement**, particularly in Kindle Unlimited (KU), where **authors are paid by the number of pages read (KENP)**. The more pages a reader consumes—and the more consistently they do so across the user base—the higher the title's performance in KU rankings and the more likely it is to be promoted in Amazon's KU-specific visibility channels.

This is where **pacing** becomes paramount. Stories that lag, meander, or fail to deliver consistent forward motion risk reader abandonment. In contrast, tightly written books with **short chapters, emotional tension, and structural propulsion** keep readers flipping pages. Each additional page read contributes not only to revenue but also to the book's **algorithmic favorability**.

Authors often use techniques such as:

- **Cliffhanger chapter endings**: A classic tool for increasing session duration, these keep readers engaged and less likely to set the book aside.
- **Alternating viewpoints**: Common in thrillers and some romance

subgenres, switching perspectives can create suspense and momentum.

- **Unresolved emotional arcs**: Particularly effective in young adult and romance, where romantic tension or interpersonal conflict keeps the reader invested in the outcome.

These are not merely storytelling devices—they are **reader retention mechanisms**, optimized to match Amazon's engagement-based performance model.

Structural Strategies by Genre

Different genres call for different pacing conventions, and successful KDP authors tailor their structure accordingly:

- **Thrillers and Mysteries**: Often feature **short, punchy chapters**, each ending with a revelation or question that drives the narrative forward. The use of **multiple POVs** or timeline shifts can heighten suspense.
- **Romance**: Relies heavily on **unresolved tension**—romantic, sexual, or interpersonal—to keep readers emotionally engaged. Cliffhangers often involve an interrupted kiss, a miscommunication, or a rival's appearance.
- **Young Adult (YA)**: Shares many of the techniques of romance and thriller—fast pacing, emotional stakes, and frequent plot twists—crafted in a tone that mirrors the immediacy of teenage experience.

In each case, the structural decisions are guided by a single objective: **maximize reader satisfaction and reading time**, thereby increasing the chances of favorable reviews, full reads in KU, and sequels purchased— data points Amazon's algorithm reads as indicators of product quality and relevance.

The Feedback Loop of Engagement

When a book combines a strong opening with sustained pacing, it triggers a **virtuous cycle** in Amazon's ecosystem:

1. **A compelling sample read leads to a sale**, improving the book's conversion rate.
2. **Engaging pacing ensures that readers read farther and longer**, increasing total KENP and session duration.
3. **Positive reader metrics lead to more algorithmic promotion**, such as being included in "Also Bought" or KU feature carousels.
4. **Higher visibility results in more downloads and reads**, reinforcing the book's algorithmic value.

This cycle continues to compound, especially if the author has a **series**, where each finished book leads naturally into the next. Readers who binge a series in KU are particularly valuable, and Amazon rewards such behavior with greater exposure across the platform.

Conclusion

In the algorithm-governed world of Amazon KDP, **readers vote with their time, not just their wallets.** Authors who understand this shift design their books not just to tell a story, but to **capture and sustain attention from the first page onward**. Strong hooks convert browsers into buyers; tight pacing turns buyers into finishers; and high reader engagement turns finishers into algorithmic ambassadors. The result is a system where story mechanics—far more than literary style—determine visibility, success, and income. To win on Amazon, an author must write for the reader's attention span, because **what hooks the reader also hooks the algorithm.**

12

Compounding Visibility

The Strategic Power of Series and Serialization in Amazon KDP

In the digital-first publishing environment of Amazon Kindle Direct Publishing (KDP), the structure and release strategy of your work are as important as the content itself. Among the most powerful levers for discoverability and sustained revenue is the decision to write a **series**. While standalone novels can succeed, KDP authors who publish interconnected books—either as a continuous narrative or thematically linked installments—are better positioned to capture long-term algorithmic favor. **Series writing is not only a storytelling technique but a visibility strategy.**

Series as an Algorithmic Asset

Amazon's recommendation engine is fueled by **data on user behavior**, and series inherently produce more of that data. When a reader finishes Book One and purchases Book Two, the algorithm detects a **sequential purchase pattern**. This chain reaction, repeated across thousands of readers, becomes a powerful signal to Amazon that the series is providing **ongoing reader satisfaction**. As a result, Amazon responds by:

- Featuring Book Two in the **"Customers Also Bought"** section of Book One,
- Placing Books Three and Four in email campaigns sent to previous buyers,
- Boosting the entire series in **genre recommendation carousels** and "related to items you've viewed" placements.

This internal promotional network effectively turns the series into a **self-reinforcing ecosystem**, where each new reader increases the visibility of the entire collection. In Amazon's algorithmic logic, **series are low-risk, high-return products**: if Book One hooks a reader, the likelihood of further purchases is significantly higher than with a standalone title.

Reader Retention and Lifetime Value

From a business perspective, a well-constructed series **maximizes customer lifetime value (CLV)**. A reader who enjoys a standalone novel provides a one-time purchase and possibly a review. A reader who invests in a series becomes a repeat buyer and often a long-term fan. In Kindle Unlimited (KU), this is especially potent: each book in a series increases the likelihood of **repeat KENP reads**, which amplifies revenue and improves the visibility of subsequent books.

Moreover, the series format facilitates **deep reader immersion**, which tends to result in stronger reviews and word-of-mouth recommendations. These reader behaviors feed back into the algorithm, which prioritizes books that generate consistent engagement over time.

Strategic Entry Points: Permafree and Low-Priced Book Ones

A proven tactic among high-performing KDP authors is to make the **first book in the series free or $0.99**. This "loss leader" strategy removes friction from the purchase decision, allowing readers to sample the series risk-free. The goal is to **funnel large numbers of readers into the series**, with the expectation that satisfied readers will continue on to the paid installments. When executed well, this model can create significant momentum:

- The free or discounted Book One garners a high volume of downloads,
- Positive engagement boosts its rank in the **"Top Free"** or **"Hot New Releases"** lists,
- Amazon's algorithm surfaces the next books in the series to these readers through **"Continue the Series"** prompts or personalized emails.

Authors who consistently deliver on the promise of Book One can rely on **organic read-through** as a stable source of sales and KU reads, effectively turning the series into a **self-sustaining engine of algorithmic exposure**.

Serialization and Release Cadence

Another key component of series strategy is **release frequency**. Amazon's algorithm strongly favors **recent releases**, often promoting them through "Hot New Releases" lists and notifying prior buyers through email alerts. Authors who publish series installments at **regular intervals (e.g., every 30–90 days)** keep their name and their books consistently in front of readers. This practice has multiple benefits:

- Each new book **refreshes interest** in previous installments,
- Frequent publication builds **anticipation and reader loyalty**,
- New releases trigger **algorithmic promotion** and visibility spikes, which can lift the entire series.

Many top-earning KDP authors use serialized publishing models to **dominate narrow genre niches,** releasing short-to-medium length novels or novellas on a rapid schedule. This not only meets reader demand but keeps the algorithm in a state of constant reinforcement.

Genre Consistency and Reader Expectations

Series success also depends on **genre coherence**. Amazon's recommendation engine clusters titles by genre, and readers build expectations around familiar tropes, tones, and character arcs. Authors who maintain consistency in genre and style—whether writing epic fantasy sagas, cozy mystery trilogies, or contemporary romance arcs—are rewarded with **algorithmic clarity**: the system knows how to categorize and whom to recommend their books to.

Breaking genre expectations mid-series (e.g., shifting from romance to paranormal thriller) can disrupt both reader loyalty and algorithmic targeting. Therefore, authors aiming for series-driven success on KDP are best served by **building a predictable, satisfying narrative environment**, book after book.

Conclusion

Series and serialization are not merely creative decisions—they are **strategic imperatives** in Amazon's algorithm-centric publishing marketplace. A well-executed series multiplies sales, enhances reader retention, and generates the behavioral data that drives Amazon's recommendation engine. From permafree entry points to structured release schedules and genre coherence, the best KDP authors understand that each book is not an island but a **node in a network of reader engagement**. When interconnected properly, that network becomes a **self-sustaining loop of visibility, satisfaction, and success**—the very conditions Amazon's algorithms are designed to reward.

13

Writing to Market

Genre Conventions, Reader Expectations, and Algorithmic Alignment in Amazon KDP

In Amazon's Kindle Direct Publishing (KDP) ecosystem, where algorithms determine discoverability and reader behavior drives rankings, one of the most powerful levers for sustained success is a writer's **ability to understand and deliver on genre expectations**. While originality and creative expression remain integral to the authorial process, those elements must be balanced with **predictable genre conventions** if a book is to thrive within Amazon's algorithmic structure.

The reason is simple: **Amazon's algorithm does not "read" books—it interprets data signals** derived from consumer behavior. These include clicks, conversions, page reads, reviews, refunds, and purchases of related titles. All of these indicators are inextricably tied to whether the book delivers the kind of reading experience its target audience anticipates. When a book aligns with reader expectations, satisfaction increases. When it violates genre norms without sufficient payoff, readers disengage—and the algorithm takes notice.

Reader Expectations as Algorithmic Currency

Every genre comes with **tacit rules**—tropes, tones, pacing, emotional arcs—that readers are conditioned to expect. These conventions are not limitations; rather, they are signals of narrative satisfaction, built from repeated exposure to works in the same category. For instance:

- A **romance** novel is expected to deliver emotional tension, romantic development, and most critically, a **happily-ever-after (HEA)** or at least a happy-for-now (HFN) ending. Without this closure, readers may feel betrayed.
- A **thriller** or **mystery** must offer escalating suspense, twists, and a clear resolution to the central conflict—often a reveal or confrontation.
- A **cozy mystery** needs to be low on graphic violence and high on quirky settings, likable amateur sleuths, and community-oriented plots.
- A **fantasy** reader expects immersive world-building, clear stakes, and often a hero's journey arc that culminates in triumph or transformation.

Authors who fulfill these expectations not only retain readers but **encourage behaviors the algorithm rewards**: full reads, sequels purchased, positive reviews, and reduced return rates. As Coverrater notes, **"books that 'match their genre expectations' tend to convert better and attract the right audience"**—and that alignment drives Amazon's internal logic for whom to recommend the book to next.

Invisible Genre Classification by Amazon

Amazon does not rely solely on author-input metadata (categories and keywords) to determine a book's genre. Instead, it uses **machine learning to perform an "invisible genre classification,"** analyzing signals like:

- The book's **cover design** (typography, color palette, imagery),
- The **title and subtitle wording,**

- The **book description and tropes mentioned,**
- Consumer behavior (what types of readers are buying and reading the book),
- And historical data on similarly performing titles.

If the book's packaging, presentation, and customer interactions all suggest "paranormal romance," for instance, the algorithm is likely to group and recommend it with other paranormal romances—even if the author listed it simply as "fantasy." This means that **genre conformity in presentation is essential.** A mismatch (e.g., a thriller with a cartoon-style cover, or a literary title mispackaged as genre fiction) may lead the algorithm to promote the book to the wrong audience, resulting in low conversion and poor engagement.

This mismatch not only weakens discoverability but can actively harm a book's trajectory. Books that generate high curiosity (e.g., from an intriguing cover) but fail to meet the genre's narrative expectations may experience **sharp drop-off in reader retention**, poor reviews, or refunds—all of which lower the book's algorithmic priority.

The Dangers of Genre Blending (and How to Do It Right)

Genre-blending can work—but only when executed with a deep understanding of **how genre expectations shape reader satisfaction.** A romance-fantasy hybrid, for example, can be highly successful if it delivers both **a coherent romantic arc** and **a richly imagined world.** However, if the romance is unresolved or the fantasy world is underdeveloped, readers from either camp may feel misled.

Books that wildly mix incompatible conventions without grounding the narrative in a **recognizable genre structure** tend to struggle. They may attract initial curiosity clicks but fail to convert or retain readers—resulting in lower visibility, higher return rates, and minimal algorithmic promotion.

The solution is not to abandon creativity, but to **"write to market"**—a strategy widely embraced among KDP authors. As defined by Self-Publishing School, writing to market means identifying what **readers in a given genre are already buying**, and then crafting stories that meet those expectations while adding fresh elements. This strategy gained popularity after the breakout success of *Twilight*, which created a massive appetite for **paranormal teen romance**. Authors who rapidly produced similar books with vampire or supernatural elements experienced a wave of sales by targeting **existing market demand with genre-consistent storytelling**.

Genre Conformity and the Feedback Loop of Success

Books that fulfill reader expectations tend to receive **more favorable reviews**, which in turn improves their conversion rate and positions them more favorably in search results and recommendations. This creates a **feedback loop**:

1. A well-packaged, genre-aligned book attracts the right readers.
2. These readers are satisfied and more likely to finish the book and buy another.
3. The algorithm notices the positive behavior and recommends the book to similar readers.
4. The book reaches more of its ideal audience, and the cycle repeats.

Conversely, a book that violates reader expectations—by subverting tropes too early, offering a jarring tonal shift, or failing to deliver expected plot resolutions—may garner negative reviews and poor completion rates, which leads the algorithm to **deprioritize** the title in discovery mechanisms.

Conclusion

In the KDP marketplace, understanding and executing **genre conventions is not a formulaic crutch—it is a strategic imperative**. Aligning your book's structure, style, tone, and packaging with genre expectations increases reader satisfaction, repeat purchases, and algorithmic discoverability. The algorithm cannot read your prose, but it can read your **reader's behavior**—and that behavior is heavily influenced by whether your story delivers what your audience subconsciously expects.

Successful KDP authors do not simply write stories—they write **market-viable products** that resonate with the algorithm's behavioral logic. The key to sustained visibility is to **thrill your ideal reader**—and that begins with meeting them where they already are: in the world of familiar, beloved, and clearly defined genre experiences.

14

Consistency as Strategy

How Release Frequency Fuels Amazon's KDP Algorithm

In Amazon's Kindle Direct Publishing (KDP) environment, timing is not incidental—it is strategic. While the quality of a book and the strength of its engagement with readers remain critical to long-term success, the **frequency and consistency of releases** play an increasingly decisive role in how a title performs within Amazon's algorithmic ecosystem. For independent authors, particularly those writing in high-volume genres like romance, fantasy, or thriller, establishing a **regular and rapid release schedule** is one of the most effective ways to maintain momentum, maximize visibility, and dominate a genre's digital shelf space.

The "Hot New Release" Window

Amazon provides all newly published books with a temporary **algorithmic advantage**. For the first **30 days** after release, a book is eligible for inclusion in the **"Hot New Releases"** list for its category. This placement offers valuable early visibility to readers who habitually browse these lists for trending content. Additionally, during this initial period, Amazon's systems give the title a **mild but meaningful promotional boost**—surfacing it in customer newsfeeds, "New for You" carousels, and email recommendations.

For authors with only one or two titles, this window is brief and finite. But for authors with a **consistent release schedule**, this promotional period can be **renewed repeatedly**, giving the appearance of continuous activity and relevance. As Reddit-based KDP discussions and genre case studies have suggested, **"Amazon's algorithms favor a release schedule of about 30 days"** for series installments. Authors who release new books every 30 to 60 days effectively remain in Amazon's spotlight year-round, with each title reinforcing the visibility of the others.

The Mechanics of Momentum

Each new release is not only a new product—it's a **new data event**. A launch can spark a surge in downloads, reviews, and "also bought" links that ripple out across your backlist. When a reader finishes Book One and sees that Book Two is already live (or about to launch), the chances of an immediate follow-up purchase or Kindle Unlimited borrow are significantly higher. This behavior triggers a valuable signal for Amazon's algorithm: **a pattern of repeat engagement**, which suggests the author is delivering satisfying content to a growing audience.

This phenomenon creates a **momentum loop**:

1. A new release gets a boost from the Hot New Releases list and new-title algorithms.
2. Existing readers of previous books purchase or read the new installment.
3. Their activity increases the visibility of the entire series or author brand.
4. New readers who discover the series are more likely to binge-read, increasing page reads and purchases across the catalogue.
5. The algorithm notices the spike in series-wide activity and continues promoting the latest book.

With each successive release, this loop becomes stronger, feeding Amazon's systems a continuous stream of favorable engagement signals.

The Rise of the "Rapid Release" Model

The most effective application of this strategy is seen in the **rapid release model**, wherein authors publish new books—especially in series—on a **monthly or bimonthly schedule**. This approach is particularly common in **high-demand genres like romance, urban fantasy, LitRPG, and cozy mystery**, where binge-reading behavior is prevalent and storylines often lend themselves to serialization.

To facilitate this strategy, authors often:

- **Write shorter novels or novellas** (40,000–60,000 words) to reduce production time,
- **Prewrite several books in a series** before releasing the first installment, allowing for regular publication without long writing gaps,
- **Break long-form narratives into episodes**, releasing them in installments to maintain continuity and maximize reader retention.

While rapid releasing is not strictly a narrative choice, it heavily influences **how authors structure their work**, including plot pacing, cliffhanger endings, and serial arcs that span multiple volumes.

Risks and Sustainability

Despite its effectiveness, the rapid release model is **not without risk**. The demands of frequent publication can lead to burnout, reduced editorial quality, and creative fatigue. Furthermore, readers may become less responsive over time if new releases feel rushed or derivative. Thus, the goal is to **balance frequency with quality**, ensuring each installment delivers a satisfying reading experience while maintaining the momentum necessary to remain visible.

Authors who succeed with this model often develop a **production pipeline**—including editing, cover design, and pre-release marketing—well in advance of publication. Many also **coordinate preorders**, which allow Amazon to collect early sales data and generate buzz in the lead-up to launch day.

The Algorithm Rewards Consistency

Amazon's algorithm is inherently reactive: it prioritizes books and authors who demonstrate **consistent engagement** with readers. Authors who release on a regular cadence are viewed as **reliable content producers**, and Amazon's systems respond by:

- Highlighting new releases in customer-specific marketing emails,
- Including the author in the **"Followed Authors"** feed (with notifications for new books),
- Featuring the newest titles in **KU recommendations** and "New & Noteworthy" carousels.

In this context, **consistency is algorithmic currency**. Even if an individual book underperforms, a steady stream of releases increases the likelihood of a breakout hit—at which point Amazon's systems begin surfacing the entire backlist to newly interested readers.

Conclusion

In the fast-moving and data-driven world of KDP publishing, success is not solely a function of what you write—it's also a function of **how and when you release it**. A consistent publishing schedule, particularly in series format, amplifies visibility, deepens engagement, and feeds the recommendation algorithms with the very behaviors they are designed to reward. While not every author can—or should—release monthly, **strategic consistency in output remains one of the most reliable ways to grow**

and sustain a publishing career on Amazon. Every new book is not just a product—it is a signal, a boost, and a new opportunity to tell the algorithm: *this author delivers, and readers want more.*

IV

Metadata, Keywords, and Categories for Discoverability

"Metadata, Keywords, and Categories for Discoverability" explores how Amazon's algorithm relies on author-supplied data to identify, classify, and recommend books. *"Metadata is the Infrastructure"* emphasizes that titles, subtitles, descriptions, and series fields form the foundation of algorithmic understanding. *"Smart Targeting"* involves choosing keywords and categories that align with real reader search behavior. *"Strategic Positioning"* refers to selecting competitive categories that maximize a book's chance to chart. *"Metadata for Maximum Reach"* highlights the importance of optimizing every field to boost conversion and search relevance. Finally, *"From Indexed to Ranked"* explains how the algorithm first recognizes your book, then elevates it based on performance metrics tied to that metadata.

IV

Metadata, Keywords, and Directories for Discoverability

15

Metadata is the Infrastructure

Building Discoverability Through Search-Driven Optimization in Amazon KDP

In the algorithmic economy of Amazon Kindle Direct Publishing (KDP), the visibility of your book begins not with its content but with its **metadata**. Long before the platform can recommend, rank, or promote your title, it must first understand what your book is and who it is for. This understanding is constructed through metadata—the **structured information you supply during publication**. As Amazon operates fundamentally as a **search engine for books**, this metadata forms the **foundation of discoverability**, allowing your book to be properly indexed, surfaced in relevant search results, and placed in front of the right audience.

Amazon as a Search Engine

To succeed on Amazon, authors must understand that the platform behaves like Google for products. Its algorithm responds to **user intent expressed through search queries**, matching those queries with product listings based on relevance. According to Reedsy, **"before any ranking can happen, Amazon must index your book for relevant searches,"** and indexing depends primarily on your **metadata and selected keywords** (Reedsy.com).

If your book is not properly indexed, it will not appear in search results, no matter how compelling the writing or how beautiful the cover. Thus, metadata is not ancillary—it is **mission-critical infrastructure**. The better your metadata communicates what your book is, the more accurately Amazon can recommend it to the right readers.

Core Elements of Metadata

The metadata you provide during the KDP upload process consists of several fields, each of which plays a distinct role in shaping Amazon's understanding of your book. These include:

- **Title and Subtitle**: The most visible elements of your book's listing. Including genre-relevant keywords in the subtitle (e.g., *A Grumpy-Sunshine Small Town Romance*) can improve search relevance and conversion.
- **Series Name**: Signals continuity and allows Amazon to group your books together, promoting sequential reads.
- **Author Name**: Becomes a searchable asset as your brand develops. Consistency is key across titles.
- **Book Description**: This functions as both a **conversion tool** and an indexing signal. Including natural language keyword phrases in the first few lines can improve searchability while persuading readers to buy.
- **Categories**: You can select two BISAC categories, but KDP also allows **backend reclassification into more specific subcategories** via Author Central or support requests.
- **Keyword Slots**: Perhaps the most directly influential field for search indexing. KDP gives you **seven keyword boxes**, where you can input up to 50 characters each of searchable phrases.

All of these elements work together to provide Amazon with a **semantic and behavioral map** of your book. If they are not optimized, the algorithm cannot accurately interpret your content, resulting in lower discoverability.

Keyword Strategy: Matching Reader Intent

Effective keyword usage is about **mirroring the search language of your target audience**. As Kindlepreneur emphasizes, **"staying on top of the latest book keywords and trends on Amazon is crucial for authors looking to maximize their visibility and sales"** (Kindlepreneur.com). This requires active research, not guesswork.

Authors should ask:

- What phrases are readers actually typing into the Amazon search bar?
- Are they searching for *"enemies to lovers romance novel"* or *"romantic suspense with a military hero"*?
- In science fiction, is it *"space opera adventure"* or *"military alien invasion novel"*?

These phrases should be incorporated into:

- **Keyword slots**, using full phrases rather than single words (e.g., "witch academy fantasy" rather than "witches, fantasy, school"),
- **The subtitle or description**, where appropriate and natural,
- **Promotional copy and advertising targeting**, reinforcing discoverability outside the listing itself.

There are multiple tools available (such as Publisher Rocket) that allow authors to research keyword trends, estimate search volume, and identify low-competition opportunities—giving self-published authors an empirical advantage.

Metadata Optimization as Ongoing Practice

Metadata is not a "set-it-and-forget-it" task. Keywords that were highly effective at launch may become saturated or outdated. Trends shift—genre language evolves, new tropes emerge, and reader preferences change.

Successful authors **regularly audit and update their metadata** to reflect current demand and positioning opportunities.

For example, a book originally published as "a fantasy novel" might be re-optimized later as "a portal fantasy adventure for fans of Sarah J. Maas," if that aligns more closely with shifting reader queries. This kind of dynamic optimization can significantly improve mid- and long-tail discoverability, especially for backlist titles.

The Consequences of Poor Metadata

Failing to optimize metadata can render an otherwise excellent book invisible. Without clear, relevant keyword associations and category alignment, Amazon's search and recommendation algorithms cannot **match the book to relevant shoppers**. The result is a listing that underperforms in search rankings, garners fewer clicks, and ultimately struggles to convert interest into sales or reads.

Moreover, **misleading or mismatched metadata**—such as placing a dark fantasy novel in the "teen & young adult" category without adjusting tone or presentation—can generate reader dissatisfaction, poor reviews, and returns. This negative feedback loop undermines both visibility and long-term platform reputation.

Conclusion

Metadata is the **linguistic infrastructure** of digital publishing on Amazon. It translates the creative essence of your book into data the algorithm can understand and act upon. Optimizing your title, description, keywords, and categories ensures that Amazon can accurately index, display, and promote your book to the readers most likely to value it. In a marketplace governed by visibility, **strategic metadata is not just beneficial—it is foundational**. Without it, even the best stories may remain undiscovered.

16

Smart Targeting

Mastering Keywords and Categories for KDP Discoverability

Amazon's Kindle Direct Publishing (KDP) platform operates not just as a bookstore, but as a **data-driven search engine**, and your book's discoverability depends heavily on how well you target that system. Among the most powerful—and frequently misunderstood—tools in an author's control are the **seven keyword slots** and **category selections** provided during the publication process. When used strategically, these elements act as **search beacons**, signaling to Amazon's algorithm how to position your book in front of the right readers. When ignored or poorly implemented, they can leave your book buried under the digital weight of better-optimized competitors.

Keywords: Your Book's Invisible Sales Force

Amazon allows authors to enter **seven keyword phrases**, each up to 50 characters, during the KDP setup. These keywords do not appear on the book's public page, but they are integral to Amazon's **search and categorization functions**. As SelfPublishingReview.com emphasizes, these keywords are what Amazon's algorithm uses to **match your book to reader queries**, making them a direct determinant of your book's visibility in search results.

Effective KDP authors maximize these keyword fields by balancing **broad searchability** with **niche relevance**. The most successful strategies avoid overly clever or idiosyncratic terms in favor of **clear, genre-signaling phrases**. For example:

- Instead of "A Tale of Urban Darkness," use "gritty urban fantasy thriller."
- Rather than "Love in the Highlands," try "Scottish historical romance."

These types of phrases help Amazon immediately classify your book by **genre, tone, setting, and subgenre**, thus connecting you with readers already looking for that specific experience.

The Power of Genre-Descriptive and Mood-Based Phrasing

The most effective keyword phrases combine **genre and emotional tone**, helping the algorithm place your book in the reader's mental and emotional frame of reference. Consider the difference between "romance" and "small-town clean romance." The former is overly broad and hypercompetitive; the latter targets a **specific reader preference** that is both emotionally coded (clean, comforting) and market-aware (small-town subgenre).

As SelfPublishingReview.com advises, incorporating mood/genre combinations like:

- "gritty detective mystery"
- "enemies to lovers dark romance"
- "lighthearted romantic comedy"

allows your book to show up in more precise search results and to resonate better with the readers who find it. This improves not just discoverability, but **conversion rate**, which is another metric Amazon tracks for ongoing promotion.

Keywords and Category Expansion: Hidden Visibility Levers

An often-overlooked but critical function of keywords is their ability to **slot your book into additional subcategories beyond the two you manually select**. According to Kindlepreneur.com, Amazon's algorithm cross-references keyword content to determine if your book qualifies for placement in other relevant genre lists. For instance:

- Using the keyword **"vampire"** can place your title in the *Fantasy > Paranormal > Vampire* subcategory, even if you didn't select it explicitly.
- Including **"cozy mystery"** can help slot your book into the *Mystery > Cozy > Women Sleuths* list.
- "Alien invasion" may trigger placement in *Science Fiction > First Contact.*

This hidden mechanism is critical because **Amazon's subcategories are where most discoverability happens**, especially for indie authors. A high rank in a niche subcategory is exponentially more valuable than being invisible in a broad category like "Romance" or "Science Fiction." Thus, **carefully optimizing your keywords can expand your categorical footprint**, giving you more opportunities to rank, chart, and be recommended.

Strategic Keyword Construction: Best Practices

To fully leverage your keyword slots, follow these best practices:

- **Use full phrases**, not single words: "post-apocalyptic survival thriller" is more effective than "apocalypse, survival, thriller."
- **Avoid repetition**: Don't duplicate terms already in your title, subtitle,

or series name—Amazon already indexes those.

- **Write like a reader**: Think about what readers would type into the search bar, not what authors or critics might call your book.
- **Focus on tropes and subgenres**: Terms like "reverse harem fantasy," "time travel romance," or "cozy holiday mystery" speak directly to niche reader interests.
- **Regularly update**: Keyword effectiveness changes over time. What's trending today may be irrelevant in six months. Revisit your metadata periodically.

Tools like Publisher Rocket, Google Trends, and even Amazon's own autofill search bar can help you gauge the popularity and competitiveness of keyword phrases, providing a data-driven edge to your strategy.

Categories: Manual and Algorithmic Placement

While Amazon allows you to manually select **two primary categories**, these are not the only categories where your book may appear. Through a combination of keyword optimization and Amazon's internal classification algorithms, your book can be listed in **multiple additional subcategories**.

Some authors also submit category update requests via **Amazon Author Central or KDP support** to access ultra-specific subcategories not available in the KDP dashboard. These granular listings often have fewer competing titles and provide better opportunities for becoming a **bestseller in category**, even with modest sales volume.

Conclusion

In the data-centric world of KDP publishing, **keywords and categories are not supplemental—they are foundational.** They tell Amazon who your audience is, what your book delivers, and where it should be placed. Smart keyword optimization can extend your reach across Amazon's marketplace, improve your rank in niche subcategories, and increase your visibility to the exact readers looking for a book like yours. Every successful KDP author treats keywords and categories not as an afterthought, but as **a precision tool for algorithmic alignment**. When executed well, this strategy makes your book discoverable, recommendable, and—ultimately—sellable.

17

Strategic Positioning

Choosing the Right Categories for Amazon KDP Success

In Amazon Kindle Direct Publishing (KDP), visibility is not evenly distributed—it is earned through algorithmic recognition, sales velocity, and precise marketplace positioning. One of the most underestimated tools in this ecosystem is the **category selection** process. When publishing a book, authors are given the option to choose up to **three categories** from Amazon's vast hierarchy of browse categories. This decision, while seemingly straightforward, has a profound impact on a book's discoverability, competitiveness, and likelihood of earning Amazon bestseller status.

As Kindlepreneur emphatically states, **"The Amazon book categories you choose will directly affect whether or not you become an Amazon bestselling author... Choose the right one, and you could become a daily bestseller with minimal marketing"** (Kindlepreneur.com). The truth behind this claim lies in the structure of Amazon's categorization system—and the way sales rank is calculated within it.

Category Rankings: A Relative Game

Amazon's category bestseller lists are not determined by absolute sales numbers but by **relative sales rank** within a given category. In other words, a book becomes a **#1 Best Seller** in a category if it is currently outselling all other books in that specific category, regardless of how competitive the broader market may be.

This structure creates a unique opportunity: a book that sells 20 copies a day might **never breach the top 1,000** in a broad, high-volume category like *Fantasy > Epic Fantasy*, but could **easily rank #1 or #2** in a more narrowly defined niche such as *Fantasy > Sword & Sorcery* or *Fantasy > Mythology > Norse*. Achieving this ranking earns the book the orange "**#1 Best Seller**" badge, boosts its visibility in the category's best-seller lists, and significantly increases its **click-through rate, credibility, and conversion**.

Broad vs. Niche Categories: Know the Trade-Off

When authors choose **broad categories**, they benefit from increased exposure to a wider audience, but also face **stiff competition** from established bestsellers, traditionally published juggernauts, and highly rated books with hundreds or thousands of reviews. Unless a book has significant marketing support or preexisting readership, it is likely to be **buried beneath higher-ranked titles**.

By contrast, selecting **niche or granular categories** reduces the sales volume needed to reach the top 10 or even #1. While these categories may attract fewer organic browsers overall, their reduced competition makes them **strategic launching pads** for early algorithmic traction. Importantly, high ranking in any category improves **cross-platform promotion**, such as email placements, homepage carousels, and the "Top in Category" recommendations.

The Mechanics of Category Selection

When publishing through KDP, the initial category options are drawn from a **simplified list mapped from BISAC (Book Industry Standards and Communications) codes**. However, Amazon's full category tree is far more granular, and authors can request additional or alternative categories by:

1. **Contacting KDP Support directly**, specifying the exact path of the desired category (e.g., *Books > Science Fiction & Fantasy > Science Fiction > Cyberpunk*),
2. **Using keyword optimization** to trigger placement in hidden categories (see previous chapter),
3. **Monitoring competitor books** to reverse-engineer which categories are active and achievable.

Some authors even combine category selection with strategic keyword placement to ensure their books land in **three or more visible categories**, beyond the standard limit.

Researching Category Opportunities

Strategic authors do not guess their way through this process. Instead, they use tools like **Publisher Rocket**, category tracking software, or manual Amazon browsing to evaluate:

- The number of books currently listed in a category,
- The average sales rank of the top 10 books in that category,
- The number of daily sales needed to hit or maintain top 10 placement,
- The presence of "#1 Best Seller" tags on competitive titles.

By comparing this data to their own realistic sales projections, authors can **target categories where their book has a viable chance of charting**. In many cases, becoming a #1 bestseller in a well-chosen niche category requires as few as **15–30 sales in a single day**, which can be achieved with a small email list, paid advertising push, or BookBub feature.

Why Category Ranking Matters

Beyond the aesthetic and psychological benefits of the orange **#1 Best Seller** badge, category ranking triggers several **practical algorithmic benefits**:

- Placement in **Amazon's top-selling lists** for that category,
- Increased inclusion in **"Also Bought" and "Recommended for You"** feeds,
- Enhanced **customer trust and conversion rates**, especially for newer or lesser-known authors,
- Potential visibility in **Amazon's marketing emails**, which feature best-selling books by genre.

These outcomes are not guaranteed by marketing spend or literary quality— they are tied directly to the book's **category-relative performance**, which can be optimized through smart categorization.

Conclusion

In the competitive environment of Amazon KDP, visibility is earned not only through content but through **positioning**. Strategic category selection allows authors to compete on realistic terms, dominate niche markets, and earn algorithmic attention with minimal external input. Whether you are launching a debut novel or managing a backlist of series titles, understanding and manipulating the category architecture of Amazon is essential to maximizing discoverability and sales. Every category you choose is a competitive arena—so choose wisely, **target where you can win**, and let Amazon's system do the rest.

18

Metadata for Maximum Reach

Fine-Tuning Every Detail for Algorithmic Precision and Reader Conversion

In Amazon Kindle Direct Publishing (KDP), **metadata is more than a technical requirement—it is a strategic asset**. While keywords and categories form the core of discoverability, **every metadata field you input contributes to Amazon's algorithmic understanding of your book**. From your subtitle to your series title, from author name to description, each element plays a role in helping Amazon determine what your book is, who it's for, and where it should appear in the marketplace. Optimizing this metadata not only enhances visibility but also improves conversion—the essential second step that turns browsers into buyers.

The Book Description: More Than Just Sales Copy

The book description, or "blurb," is often the **first point of persuasion** after a potential reader lands on your product page. It must accomplish two tasks: **convert the reader's curiosity into a purchase** and **signal content relevance to Amazon's algorithm**. While Amazon gives greater algorithmic weight to keywords, title, and subtitle, it **does index some**

content from the description, especially when keywords appear naturally and contextually.

According to Coverrater.com, **a keyword-rich description reinforces genre relevance**, which helps guide the algorithm toward correct audience placement. For example, a blurb that uses phrases like "dark enemies-to-lovers romance," "post-apocalyptic survival," or "time-travel historical fantasy" not only appeals to reader expectations but confirms the book's identity to Amazon's search and recommendation engines.

Furthermore, the description directly influences your **conversion rate**. A compelling, genre-aware blurb can dramatically increase the percentage of page views that result in sales or downloads—a metric Amazon tracks and uses to determine whether a book deserves wider exposure. Simply put, **strong descriptions enhance sales performance, and sales performance powers visibility**.

Subtitle and Series Fields: Metadata's Hidden Powerhouses

While the title is often fixed by branding or thematic considerations, the **subtitle field is a flexible and underutilized asset**. Amazon allows subtitles of up to 200 characters, and within that space, authors can include key genre signals, tropes, and thematic phrases. For example:

Title: Echoes of the Past

Subtitle: A Medieval Time-Travel Fantasy Romance with a Warrior Heroine and a Dangerous Secret

This subtitle achieves several objectives:

- It clarifies genre and subgenre,
- It embeds **multiple searchable terms,**
- It appeals directly to reader expectations.

Likewise, the **series field** links books together, helping Amazon understand relational data. A clearly titled and consistently used series name (e.g., *The Starborn Chronicles*) allows the algorithm to promote books in order, place "Book Two" in the "Customers Also Bought" of "Book One," and deliver email notifications when new installments go live. It also boosts **read-through potential**, which Amazon heavily favors as a sales amplifier.

Author Name: Brand Consistency and Discoverability

Though often overlooked, your **author name itself is a metadata signal**. For established brands or pen names, readers may search by author, and Amazon uses this to generate "More by This Author" carousels and curated recommendations. Ensuring that your author name is spelled and styled consistently across all titles is essential for maintaining **algorithmic linkage**.

If you're writing in different genres under separate pen names, this becomes even more critical. Misalignment here can confuse both readers and the system, resulting in irrelevant recommendations or poor audience targeting.

Supporting Metadata: Accuracy Enables Discovery

Amazon uses every metadata input to **refine its recommendation and search matching algorithms**, including:

- **Language**: Ensures the book is offered to readers based on their language preference settings.
- **Age and Grade Range**: Essential for children's and young adult books. Incorrect settings here may result in your book being marketed to the wrong audience—or hidden from the right one.
- **Mature Content Tags**: If applicable, failing to label adult content properly can restrict or misplace your book, limiting its exposure in both search and browse functions.

As Book Boss Academy emphasizes, **Amazon's algorithm is designed to**

"show books to the right readers" based on how authors categorize them. Misclassification—whether intentional or accidental—can result in lower engagement, higher return rates, and poor visibility. Accurate metadata not only avoids these pitfalls but improves **reader satisfaction**, which translates into better reviews, higher rankings, and enhanced long-term discoverability.

Metadata as a System, Not a Checkbox

The various metadata elements—title, subtitle, series, author name, description, keywords, and categories—do not work in isolation. They function as an **interconnected metadata ecosystem**, each reinforcing the signals sent by the others. When all elements are aligned—title matches keywords, description echoes subtitle, series name links backlist titles—the algorithm receives a **clear, confident signal about your book's identity and audience fit**.

In contrast, inconsistencies—such as a mismatched subtitle, vague description, or unrelated keywords—send mixed signals, which can confuse the algorithm and reduce the book's visibility across Amazon's search, browse, and recommendation functions.

Conclusion

Metadata optimization is not simply a technical step in the publishing process—it is a **core discipline of digital authorship**. Every field on the KDP dashboard presents an opportunity to improve visibility, accuracy, and conversion. From compelling, keyword-smart descriptions to strategically structured subtitles and series names, each element contributes to the algorithm's ability to match your book with its ideal readers.

Success in the KDP marketplace is not just about writing a great book. It is about making sure the **system understands that it's great—and knows exactly who to show it to**. When metadata is done right, it becomes your silent marketer: targeting, positioning, and promoting your book 24/7 within Amazon's global platform.

19

From Indexed to Ranked

Mastering Amazon's Search Algorithm Through Metadata and Performance

Publishing on Amazon Kindle Direct Publishing (KDP) is not simply about creating a book—it is about positioning that book in a search-driven, algorithmically ranked marketplace. While crafting effective metadata is crucial to ensure your book is *indexed*—that is, recognized and included in relevant search results—the next critical step is winning the *ranking* game. Ranking determines **how high your book appears** when shoppers search for terms like *"space opera science fiction"* or *"gritty detective mystery."* On Amazon, visibility depends on not just showing up, but showing up **first**—and to do that, you must understand how Amazon's search algorithm evaluates and ranks indexed content.

Indexing: The First Threshold

Before your book can compete for visibility, it must first be properly **indexed** for the search terms that matter. Indexing means that Amazon has recognized your book as relevant to a particular keyword or phrase, based on your metadata—specifically your **title, subtitle, series name,**

book description, and keyword slots. As Matthew J. Holmes explains, **"the search algorithm considers relevance (do the query terms match your metadata?)"** (Holmes, 2023). If a reader searches for *"military sci-fi alien invasion,"* and your book contains that phrase or its components in the metadata, it becomes eligible to appear in the results.

This is why keyword research and placement during setup are foundational: **metadata gets your book into the game.** But once you're in the indexed pool, you must outperform other books to rise in the rankings.

Ranking: The Real Competition

Amazon's algorithm doesn't rank books solely by how well they match a search query. Once indexed, books are ordered in search results based on a combination of **relevance and performance**. Two performance metrics dominate this calculation:

1. **Conversion Rate** – What percentage of users who view your book end up purchasing it?
2. **Sales Velocity** – How many copies are sold (or Kindle Unlimited pages read) within a short time window?

If your book is indexed for *"space opera science fiction"* and people **consistently click and purchase** your book when they search that term, the algorithm interprets this as a strong match. As Holmes notes, **"if your book starts selling well to people who search that term, Amazon will rank you higher for those searches going forward."** The search engine learns from buyer behavior—what it ranks higher gets more clicks, and what gets more clicks and conversions climbs higher still.

This creates a **feedback loop**:

• Higher ranking → More visibility → More clicks and sales → Higher ranking.

This loop also means that **early-stage momentum is critical.** If your book gains traction for a key search term within the first days or weeks of launch, Amazon may start featuring it more prominently—potentially leading to sustained organic traffic for months.

Strategic Keyword Targeting and Traffic Generation

To trigger this positive cycle, savvy authors **combine precise metadata with targeted promotional efforts.** Simply inserting a keyword into your metadata isn't enough—you must **drive traffic** that converts.

For example, if *"alien space marine adventure"* is one of your primary keyword targets:

- Ensure it appears in your keyword slot and is echoed in your subtitle or description.
- Use **Amazon Ads (Sponsored Products)** targeting that exact keyword.
- Run **discount or launch promotions** to spike downloads for that keyword search.

When Amazon sees that people searching *"alien space marine adventure"* are clicking and buying your book more than the competition, it flags your listing as **high-performing for that search term**. Over time, this improves your organic rank for that phrase, reducing your reliance on paid traffic and increasing sustainable visibility.

The Role of Refinement and Ongoing Optimization

Amazon's marketplace is dynamic. New trends emerge, reader interests evolve, and keywords that were once dominant may fade. Therefore, metadata optimization is not a "set and forget" task—it must be treated as **an iterative process**.

KDP allows you to update your:

- **Keyword slots**
- **Book description**
- **Categories (through support or Author Central)**

While changes may take several days to propagate across Amazon's system, timely updates allow you to **ride emerging keyword trends**, keep your listings relevant, and capture new waves of search traffic. For example, if *"academy magic romance"* suddenly trends in your genre, updating your metadata to include that term can get your book indexed and potentially ranked for it—if paired with smart promotional traffic.

This agile approach gives indie authors a competitive edge over traditional publishers, who often set metadata once and rarely revisit it. As Holmes stresses, **"good metadata opens the door, and good performance secures your place."**

Conclusion

Success in Amazon's marketplace is a two-stage battle: **first for inclusion, then for prominence.** Metadata—your keywords, categories, title, subtitle, and description—gets your book *indexed* and discoverable. But only by generating strong engagement through high conversion rates and sales velocity can you *rank* and sustain visibility. Smart authors use data-driven keyword targeting, strategic launch promotions, and ongoing optimization to secure and maintain high rankings for profitable search terms.

Amazon's algorithm is ruthlessly rational: it rewards books that attract and satisfy buyers for specific queries. Your goal, then, is to ensure that when a reader types in the phrase you're targeting, **your book not only shows up—but sells.**

V

Market Trends and Topics Influencing Recommendations

"Market Trends and Topics Influencing Recommendations" examines how Amazon's algorithm reacts to evolving reader demand, rewarding authors who align their content with what the market actively seeks. *"Writing to Market vs. Chasing Trends"* distinguishes strategic alignment from short-lived opportunism, while *"Navigating the Trend Currents"* explores how to capitalize on rising tropes without sacrificing quality. *"Market-Driven Non-Fiction"* reveals how timely topics—like political biographies or true crime—can surge in visibility. *"Harnessing Seasonal and Niche Trends"* highlights predictable spikes tied to holidays or hobbies. *"Responding to the Market"* addresses the algorithm's sensitivity to viral influence and off-platform buzz, and *"Longevity vs. Flash-in-the-Pan"* reminds authors that sustained success comes from blending trend appeal with enduring genre fundamentals.

20

Writing to Market vs. Chasing Trends

Strategic Alignment in the KDP Marketplace

In the ever-evolving Amazon Kindle Direct Publishing (KDP) ecosystem, the difference between long-term success and fleeting visibility often hinges on a critical distinction: *writing to market* versus *chasing trends*. Both approaches aim to align a book with what readers are currently seeking, but only one offers sustainable, repeatable results in the context of Amazon's algorithmic logic and genre dynamics.

This chapter explores that distinction, drawing on insights from publishing experts and historical case studies to illuminate how authors can make strategically sound decisions about what to write—and when.

Writing to Market: Strategic Alignment with Reader Demand

At its core, *writing to market* means crafting a book with a deliberate awareness of what readers want—based on genre conventions, proven demand, and prevailing themes. According to **Self-Publishing School**, writing to market involves entering genres or subgenres that have:

- A large and actively engaged readership,
- Clear reader expectations and buying behavior,
- A track record of consistent commercial success.

This approach does not require sacrificing originality or creativity. Rather, it means shaping your creative output around **existing demand** rather than purely artistic impulse. For example, authors who enter the cozy mystery, clean romance, or domestic thriller markets with a solid grasp of those genres' tropes and tone are more likely to gain traction because Amazon already has a **well-trained recommendation system** built around those categories.

Importantly, books that "write to market" tend to be easier for Amazon's algorithm to classify and promote. They fit neatly into established consumer behavior patterns, which means the algorithm can confidently recommend them to relevant shoppers. This alignment maximizes the likelihood of positive metrics: higher click-through rates (CTR), stronger conversion rates, and greater read-through—all of which feed the system's ranking and visibility mechanisms.

Chasing Trends: High Risk, Volatile Reward

In contrast, *chasing trends* refers to writing content that attempts to capitalize on **sudden spikes in consumer interest**, often driven by current events, pop culture, or viral media. While this can result in rapid visibility and sales if timed well, it carries substantial risks.

Self-Publishing School highlights a prominent example: the *paranormal teen romance* boom that followed the success of *Twilight*. During this period, authors who released vampire or werewolf-themed romances experienced strong sales because demand was spiking. However, within a few years, **market saturation and reader fatigue** led to a dramatic cooling of the trend. Many books that might have sold well in 2011 were virtually invisible by 2014.

This phenomenon illustrates the fundamental challenge of chasing trends:

- Timing is unpredictable.
- Audience interest is often short-lived.
- The algorithm may initially amplify trend-chasing books, but long-term performance depends on sustained relevance.

Authors who chase trends without understanding **genre structure** or without writing in a market that aligns with their own storytelling strengths often struggle to maintain sales once the trend collapses.

Balancing Timeliness with Longevity

The most effective strategy for sustainable success in the KDP ecosystem is to **blend market awareness with genre fidelity**. This means:

- Identifying genres with **evergreen popularity** (e.g., romance, thrillers, self-help),
- Tracking **emerging tropes** within those genres (e.g., "grumpy-sunshine romance," "academy fantasy," "dark academia"),
- Writing books that **satisfy core genre expectations** while incorporating **timely elements** to boost discoverability.

For example, writing a small-town romance series (evergreen) that incorporates a popular trope like "forced proximity" or "second-chance love" (timely) can yield both short-term traction and long-term viability.

This approach respects the algorithm's tendency to promote **books that satisfy readers repeatedly and reliably**. A hot trope may get your book noticed initially, but only strong genre execution will keep it selling.

Conclusion: Build with Awareness, Not Reaction

The KDP marketplace is undeniably trend-sensitive, and authors who ignore market signals do so at their peril. However, chasing fleeting fads without foundational strategy is equally hazardous. Instead of reacting to what's momentarily hot, authors should *respond* to what's *consistently desired*—and write books that satisfy that demand in a timely and authentic way.

As **Self-Publishing School** advises, the key is to recognize **sustainable trends**—those that emerge within existing genre ecosystems—and to build content that both captures current attention and endures beyond the moment.

In KDP, the algorithm favors engagement. But engagement starts with alignment. *Write what readers want—when they want it—and do so in a way that respects the genre, the market, and the moment.*

21

Navigating the Trend Currents

Writing to Market Without Chasing Fads

In the fast-evolving digital marketplace of Amazon Kindle Direct Publishing (KDP), **timing, positioning, and reader alignment** are often as crucial as craft. One of the most frequently discussed strategic approaches among successful indie authors is **"writing to market"**—a method that involves tailoring a book's concept, structure, and style to align with **genres, tropes, and themes currently in high demand**. While some confuse this approach with "chasing trends," the two are conceptually distinct and carry very different implications for long-term success.

Writing to Market: Serving Known Demand

At its core, writing to market means **writing what readers are already proven to want**. It is a method rooted in pragmatic authorship: creating a book that fulfills clear audience expectations within a well-established commercial niche. As Self-Publishing School describes, **"writing to market" is about identifying genres or topics that are currently popular and crafting books that satisfy that demand** (SelfPublishingSchool.com).

This does not mean sacrificing originality. In fact, writing to market often requires an author to balance creativity with **genre conformity**, ensuring that the book delivers familiar tropes (which readers expect) while offering fresh execution (which readers appreciate). For example:

- A **paranormal romance** still needs the expected emotional beats, but the setting or creature mythos can be novel.
- A **mafia romance** benefits from the classic antihero arc but may stand out through cultural specificity or narrative complexity.

By aligning content with a known reader appetite, authors increase their chance of visibility, conversion, and positive reader engagement—the three primary metrics that drive Amazon's recommendation algorithm.

The Algorithm's Role in Market Responsiveness

Amazon's system is inherently **reactionary**. It reflects what shoppers do in real time: what they search for, click on, read, and review. When a surge of interest appears in a specific topic or subgenre—often triggered by cultural moments, viral media, or celebrity endorsements—Amazon's search and recommendation engines quickly adjust to **surface relevant content**.

As Kindlepreneur highlights, **"Amazon's algorithms are very sensitive to spikes in interest."** When readers suddenly flock to a theme like *"dark academia," "shifter romance," or "cozy witch mysteries,"* Amazon algorithmically seeks out books that match those interests and promotes them in keyword-driven search results, curated carousels, and email recommendations (Kindlepreneur.com).

Authors who anticipate or quickly respond to these trend surges are ideally positioned to **ride the wave of demand**. Their books become the algorithm's answer to new market questions. This agility can yield:

- Rapid initial exposure via "Hot New Releases" lists,
- Strong early sales velocity (a key ranking factor),
- Organic promotion through "Customers Also Bought" and genre

newsletters.

Real-Time Trends in Practice

Recent data confirms that **emerging tropes leave a visible footprint** in Amazon search behavior. Popular current examples include:

- **"Romantasy"**: a blend of fantasy and romance, often with magical kingdoms and emotionally charged relationships.
- **"Academy fantasy"**: narratives set in magical schools, typically combining young adult voice with high fantasy tropes.
- **"Shifter romance"**: often involving werewolves, dragons, or other shape-shifting beings in emotionally intense plots.
- **"Mafia romance" (particularly Bratva/Russian mafia subtypes)**: offering morally gray antiheroes and high-stakes tension.
- **"Cozy mysteries"**: especially those with culinary or cottagecore themes.

These are not fads—they are evolving **micro-markets** within larger genre ecosystems, and their presence in keyword searches indicates sustained reader interest. Books that fit neatly into these niches are more likely to be indexed, promoted, and ranked favorably by Amazon's systems.

The Danger of Chasing Trends

However, **chasing trends**—as opposed to writing to market—often leads to diminished results. Chasing a trend means rushing to produce content that simply imitates what is currently popular, often without deep understanding of the genre's mechanics or the readers' emotional expectations. This reactive approach has three critical risks:

1. **Saturation**: By the time your book is written, edited, and published, the trend may be overcrowded or fading.
2. **Inauthenticity**: Readers in niche genres have sharp genre awareness.

A book that mimics the surface of a trend but fails to deliver on the genre's emotional or narrative promises will generate poor reviews and low read-through.

3. **Brand inconsistency**: Jumping from trend to trend can prevent an author from building a loyal readership, as readers are uncertain what to expect from future releases.

In short, trend-chasing can yield short-term curiosity but rarely builds long-term visibility or profitability. The more sustainable approach is to **write to market with awareness of durable trends and genre longevity**.

Identifying Evergreen Trends

Some reader interests endure across years and cultural shifts. These are **evergreen trends**, and writing to them offers both immediate relevance and long-term sales potential. Examples include:

- Enemies-to-lovers romance,
- Found family dynamics in fantasy,
- Strong female sleuths in cozy mysteries,
- Time-travel historical adventures,
- Small-town contemporary romances.

Authors who learn to identify these deeper patterns—not just the aesthetic of the moment—are better positioned to write books that resonate over time. They align not just with current demand, but with **structural desires in the market**.

Conclusion

Writing to market is not about sacrificing creativity or pandering to trends. It is about **aligning your narrative with known reader desires** while maintaining your unique voice and perspective. The Amazon algorithm rewards books that satisfy reader expectations, and those expectations are constantly visible in real-time search behavior. The most successful KDP authors don't chase every new fad—they monitor rising interest, assess sustainability, and act swiftly but authentically when they see a viable opportunity.

When executed with skill, writing to market becomes a **scalable strategy**—one that grows your audience, builds trust with the algorithm, and creates a career that adapts to reader needs without losing artistic integrity.

22

Market-Driven Non-Fiction

Timing, Trends, and Topical Relevance in Amazon KDP

In the Amazon Kindle Direct Publishing (KDP) ecosystem, **market responsiveness is not confined to fiction.** Non-fiction, perhaps even more so than genre fiction, is **acutely sensitive to cultural, political, and media-driven shifts**, and authors who strategically align their books with real-world events can capture substantial, often sudden, reader demand. The Amazon algorithm, ever attuned to consumer behavior, reflects these surges in interest by **surfacing titles related to trending topics**, often giving visibility boosts to newly released or well-positioned books.

This phenomenon defines what is commonly referred to as **market-driven non-fiction**—books written or released in alignment with topical trends, news cycles, or public interest moments. While evergreen categories such as self-help, business, and health remain staples of non-fiction publishing, **timely releases tied to high-interest subjects can enjoy disproportionately high visibility and sales velocity**, all amplified by Amazon's recommendation systems.

Topical Relevance as an Algorithmic Trigger

Amazon's algorithms do not operate in a vacuum. They observe **search volume, sales spikes, and customer engagement** to identify trending topics, and they respond rapidly to external signals from the media and culture. As Kindlepreneur notes, when a new film, celebrity scandal, political upheaval, or public debate arises, **related search activity increases**, and Amazon begins **surfacing relevant titles** to match those queries (Kindlepreneur.com).

For example:

- In 2023, the release of *Walter Isaacson's Elon Musk biography* caused a notable surge in searches for terms like "Elon Musk biography," "SpaceX," and "tech billionaire books."
- Simultaneously, the cinematic release of *Oppenheimer* prompted increased interest in atomic science history, nuclear policy, and World War II biographies.
- Around election cycles, books about political figures, campaign strategies, and social policy experience **search-driven boosts**.

Amazon's algorithm identifies these shifts in reader interest and promotes relevant content accordingly—often including **newly released books that match trending keywords**, even if they lack a robust sales history. This **algorithmic gap-filling** means that if demand is high but the catalog is sparse, Amazon will push newer books more aggressively to meet reader curiosity.

True Crime and the Evergreen Trend Model

Not all non-fiction trends are fleeting. Some topics exhibit **long-term, high-volume search behavior** that sustains reader interest regardless of the news cycle. One such category is **true crime**, which remains a dominant force in both traditional and self-published markets.

Kindlepreneur reports that **true crime searches—particularly those involving serial killers, unsolved cases, or psychological analysis of criminals—remain persistently strong** (<u>Kindlepreneur.com</u>). Readers drawn to these topics often consume multiple books within the niche, much like fiction readers who follow a mystery series. This behavior fosters a durable market ecosystem where new titles are regularly surfaced in recommendation engines, and each book contributes to a broader web of interest around the genre.

For authors, this means that **true crime and similarly resilient categories offer a reliable baseline for sales,** while still leaving room for spike opportunities when specific cases resurface in the public eye through documentaries, podcasts, or media coverage.

Timing and Trend Synchronization

In market-driven non-fiction, **timing is critical**. Authors who can anticipate or react quickly to rising interest around a person, event, or topic are positioned to **ride algorithmic momentum**. This explains why, for instance, multiple books about a prominent figure may be released within the same month:

- Public interest is high,
- Search activity is surging,
- Amazon's algorithm is looking for content to recommend.

Each book in such a trend wave **reinforces the presence of the others,** creating a rising tide that elevates all titles. For example, readers browsing one Elon Musk book may be shown several others in the "Customers Also Bought" carousel, resulting in mutual exposure. This network effect amplifies discoverability and can **create a temporary micro-market** that delivers high conversion for a concentrated period.

For self-publishing authors, this opens up strategic pathways:

- **Rapid production of short-form non-fiction** (e.g., 15,000–30,000 word primers) on trending topics,
- **Preemptive planning** based on upcoming media events (biopics, anniversaries, elections),
- **Metadata optimization** (keywords, subtitles, descriptions) that captures trending search queries.

Challenges and Considerations

While the upside potential of market-driven non-fiction is significant, it also carries inherent risks:

- **Volatility**: Interest may vanish as quickly as it spikes, leaving a book with minimal residual traffic.
- **Saturation**: A popular trend may attract a flood of low-quality content, making it harder to stand out.
- **Research depth**: Readers of topical non-fiction expect **credibility and insight**, particularly when dealing with real people or sensitive subjects. Rushing to capitalize on a trend without rigorous sourcing can lead to reputational harm and negative reviews.

The key is **speed with integrity**—producing timely content that is accurate, well-crafted, and aligned with genuine reader interest.

Conclusion

Market-driven non-fiction presents a powerful opportunity for KDP authors willing to **observe, respond to, and align with real-world events**. Amazon's algorithm is engineered to detect trending demand and promote content that meets it. By identifying high-interest topics—whether rooted in pop culture, politics, or enduring curiosity niches like true crime—authors can position their books for maximum visibility during moments of peak engagement.

The lesson is simple but profound: **timing and topical relevance matter**. For authors in the non-fiction space, staying attuned to what readers care about *right now*—and delivering books that inform, explore, or contextualize those interests—can unlock the full promotional power of Amazon's search and recommendation systems.

23

Harnessing Seasonal and Niche Trends

Timing Content for Maximum Visibility in Amazon KDP

In the constantly shifting landscape of Amazon Kindle Direct Publishing (KDP), long-term strategy is critical—but so is **timing**. Savvy authors understand that certain types of content predictably perform better at specific points in the calendar or during cultural shifts. These **seasonal and niche trends** not only influence reader demand, but they are also **factored into Amazon's algorithmic behavior**, shaping which books are recommended, ranked, and surfaced more prominently.

By aligning your publishing schedule and marketing efforts with these temporal and cultural rhythms, you increase your book's visibility precisely when readers are most likely to be looking. Done correctly, this strategy enables you to **ride built-in demand waves**, increasing sales velocity, reader engagement, and algorithmic favor.

The Algorithm's Seasonal Sensitivity

Amazon's algorithm, driven by vast historical purchase data, **anticipates annual demand cycles** and promotes content accordingly. As the calendar approaches specific seasonal markers—such as Halloween, Thanksgiving, or Christmas—the system begins **elevating books in genres or topics that historically perform well during that period**.

For example:

- In **Q4 (October–December)**, there is a noticeable boost in visibility for:
- *Christmas-themed romances and cozy mysteries,*
- *Giftable non-fiction* (cookbooks, inspirational titles, self-improvement),
- *Children's holiday books,*
- *New Year's health and fitness content.*
- In **October**, the system begins recommending:
- *Horror and supernatural fiction,*
- *Witchy or paranormal-themed books,*
- *Halloween anthologies and dark fantasy.*

This phenomenon is not anecdotal—it's engineered. Amazon's homepage carousels, "Seasonal Picks," and genre landing pages often feature seasonal content **weeks ahead of the actual holiday**, based on internal data indicating when reader interest typically begins to rise.

For KDP authors, this means that **launching a holiday-themed book just as the season is beginning**—rather than at its peak—is key. For instance, a Christmas romance released in early November will benefit from Amazon's algorithmic push, whereas one launched mid-December may miss the marketing window entirely.

Niche Trends and Cultural Micro-Waves

Beyond predictable seasonality, **niche interest trends can also drive sudden and significant spikes in demand**, especially during times of social upheaval, media phenomena, or viral cultural events. These are more difficult to forecast but can be highly lucrative for agile authors.

Examples include:

- A spike in **bread-baking books** and cookery titles during pandemic lockdowns,
- A rise in **home organization and minimalism guides** following popular Netflix series or social trends,
- Increased demand for **travel guides and adventure memoirs** during spring and summer vacation planning seasons,
- Sudden popularity of **journaling and self-care books** after New Year's resolutions or wellness trends circulate.

These **micro-waves of demand** are often brief but intense. Authors who recognize the trend and act quickly—either by creating new content or promoting relevant backlist titles—can capitalize on this attention and benefit from the algorithm's appetite for "new and relevant" offerings.

Identifying Emerging Trends: Tools and Tactics

To position your book ahead of seasonal or niche waves, it's essential to **monitor cultural signals and Amazon-specific data**. Some proven methods include:

- **Watching Amazon's "Most Read" or "Trending Now" lists**: These are published on Amazon Charts and often hint at genre spikes or topic surges.
- **Observing search autofill and related searches**: Begin typing genre-relevant keywords into Amazon's search bar and take note of what

phrases autofill—these represent high-volume reader queries.

- **Tracking book sales calendars**: Study past trends on when seasonal content begins to climb. For example, Christmas titles begin ranking in early November, and fitness books spike in January.
- **Following media and pop culture**: Announcements of film adaptations, celebrity memoirs, or current events often foreshadow demand for related non-fiction or thematic fiction.

Staying plugged into both publishing industry chatter and Amazon's behavioral patterns allows authors to make **data-informed decisions** about what to write and when to release it.

Applying Seasonality to Marketing Strategy

Even if you are not writing entirely seasonal content, you can still **align your promotions with seasonal moods**. For example:

- Bundle a romantic novel with a "Valentine's Day" marketing angle in February.
- Promote a self-help title as part of "Back to School Reset" in late summer.
- Emphasize spooky or supernatural themes in a fantasy series for Halloween-themed advertising.

Moreover, authors with large backlists can repackage and promote older titles seasonally, using **updated metadata, Amazon Ads, or email campaigns**. By resurfacing books at the right time, you allow Amazon's algorithm to rediscover and re-rank them, even if their original release dates have long passed.

Conclusion

Seasonal and niche trends offer authors **predictable, renewable opportunities** to gain visibility and drive sales on Amazon. By understanding the algorithm's seasonal biases and the cultural forces that shape reader behavior, KDP authors can time their launches, promotions, and even writing projects to **align with waves of rising interest**. This is not manipulation—it is strategic alignment with the rhythms of consumer demand.

In a platform where visibility is half the battle, learning to publish *when* readers are searching—not just what they're searching for—is a skill that transforms passive authors into proactive entrepreneurs. **Time your book to the market, and the market will meet your book halfway.**

24

Responding to the Market: External Trends, Viral Influence, and the Algorithm's Reactive Role

In the age of real-time media, **Amazon's algorithm does not exist in isolation**. While much of its behavior is governed by internal signals—such as search volume, conversion rates, and sales velocity—**its rankings and recommendations are highly reactive to external cultural phenomena**, particularly trends that originate off-platform. In this context, a book's success is not always born within Amazon's marketplace; often, it is ignited elsewhere—on TikTok, YouTube, Instagram, or news media—and Amazon's algorithm adjusts accordingly to **amplify what readers are already chasing.**

This dynamic underscores a core truth of the Amazon ecosystem: **the algorithm doesn't start trends—it follows them.** It functions as a reflection of real-time market demand, adapting its recommendations and category visibility based on what is already attracting attention. For KDP authors, this presents both a challenge and an opportunity: the challenge is to stay agile enough to respond quickly; the opportunity lies in riding waves of external interest that can rapidly escalate into significant, algorithm-fueled sales momentum.

The TikTok Effect: When Virality Meets Velocity

No modern discussion of reader-driven influence would be complete without addressing the phenomenon of **BookTok**—a subcommunity on TikTok responsible for transforming quiet mid-list books into breakout bestsellers. One viral video showcasing a book's emotional arc, trope appeal, or aesthetic design can drive thousands of new readers to Amazon within days. This **"TikTok made me buy it"** phenomenon has demonstrably reshaped the Kindle charts in categories such as **romantasy, dark fantasy, contemporary romance, and even horror**.

Once Amazon detects a surge in search volume, clicks, and sales—especially if it occurs within a narrow window—the algorithm responds by:

- Boosting the title's **placement in "Best Seller" and "Hot New Release" lists,**
- Recommending the book in **"Customers Also Bought"** carousels for similar titles,
- Including it in **automated marketing emails** to readers with relevant purchasing histories.

As a result, a book that goes viral off-platform can see its **visibility multiply exponentially within Amazon**, even if the initial spark was entirely external. For indie authors, this underscores the importance of **monitoring not just Amazon metrics, but broader cultural currents**.

Social Media Trends and Genre Resurgence

Social media-driven surges often cause genre-level disruptions, not just individual book spikes. For instance, **the resurgence of "dark fantasy romantasy"** on TikTok led to a reordering of Kindle's fantasy and romance bestseller lists, with previously obscure titles suddenly dominating chart positions. Amazon's system responded by prioritizing romantasy-themed books across its:

- Genre landing pages,
- Also Bought loops,
- Personalized recommendations.

Such examples demonstrate that **external platforms can dictate what Amazon's algorithm surfaces**, provided that reader behavior aligns with the trend.

Authors who **anticipate or mirror these emerging aesthetics**—through cover design, keywords, or content—are more likely to benefit from this systemic reorientation. The algorithm isn't evaluating the book's style; it's reacting to the **patterns of reader interest**, and authors who understand those patterns can position their titles to be found more easily.

Tools for Trend Anticipation

To stay competitive, authors must adopt a **market-attuned mindset**, using tools and data to monitor what's gaining momentum. Recommended resources include:

- **K-lytics Reports**: These provide genre-specific sales and competition data, revealing which categories are expanding or contracting.
- **Kindlepreneur's Keyword Tools**: Helpful for identifying rising search terms and popular tropes that are beginning to trend within Amazon's ecosystem.
- **Social media monitoring**: Following BookTok, genre-specific Instagram hashtags, YouTube booktubers, and Goodreads discussions can reveal what's resonating with readers in real time.

This proactive approach allows authors to **write to market** effectively—not by cynically copying what's popular, but by aligning with existing interest in a way that feels authentic and deliverable.

Marketing as a Trend Accelerator

While the algorithm follows demand, **well-targeted external marketing can help initiate a surge** that Amazon will then amplify. Authors can leverage:

- **TikTok and Instagram Reels** to showcase aesthetic or emotional hooks,
- **Book trailers or quote graphics** to generate buzz pre-launch,
- **ARC teams and influencer partnerships** to create early momentum.

Once sales begin to accumulate, Amazon's system will detect the spike and start **promoting the book more aggressively to shoppers with matching interests**, potentially catalyzing the type of feedback loop that defines breakout success stories.

Sustainability Over Hype

That said, **not all trends are worth chasing**. Authors must be cautious not to compromise their creative integrity or reader trust by attempting to jump on every viral wave. As Self-Publishing School warns, "**chasing every fad can burn out both you and your audience**" (SelfPublishingSchool.com). The key is to identify:

- **Trends that align with your brand and writing style,**
- **Tropes and genres you can deliver with quality and consistency,**
- **Markets with enough durability to support long-term readership.**

Writing to market should never become a purely reactive exercise. Instead, it should be a deliberate alignment of authorial intent with reader desire—**an intersection of commerce and craft**.

Conclusion

Amazon's algorithm is not an initiator of trends but a powerful **amplifier of existing interest**. It reacts to the marketplace—influenced by viral content, media moments, and shifting reader preferences—by promoting books that appear to match surging demand. For KDP authors, success increasingly depends on the ability to **recognize and respond to external signals**, shaping metadata, marketing, and even book development around what readers are actively seeking.

By staying tuned into the cultural conversation and leveraging tools that track emerging interest, authors can place themselves at the forefront of algorithmic momentum. And when the market moves, **Amazon will move with it—pushing forward the books that got there first.**

25

Longevity vs. Flash-in-the-Pan

Building a Career Beyond the Trend Cycle in Amazon KDP

In the fast-moving world of Amazon Kindle Direct Publishing (KDP), success can strike suddenly—but sustaining that success requires foresight, planning, and a long-term mindset. While aligning with emerging trends can lead to a **burst of visibility and sales**, savvy authors know that the ultimate goal is not just a fleeting bestseller badge, but a **durable author brand and a profitable backlist**. Amazon's algorithm rewards trend-driven momentum, but it also privileges **consistency, reader satisfaction, and catalog depth** over time.

The key to enduring success lies in striking a **strategic balance between trend exploitation and genre mastery**—building a catalogue that benefits from waves of demand while remaining viable in calmer market waters.

The Appeal and Risks of Trend-Driven Hits

Writing to trending topics—whether it's a hot trope like "dark mafia romance" or a viral aesthetic like "academy fantasy"—can significantly accelerate a book's initial performance. A well-timed release that aligns with surging reader interest benefits from:

- Increased **search volume and visibility**,
- Higher likelihood of **appearing in Amazon's recommendation engine**,
- The potential for **viral momentum**, especially if paired with social media buzz.

However, such surges are often **short-lived**. The trend cools, the surge subsides, and sales may taper off. For authors with no follow-up plan or backlist, this can create a **boom-and-bust cycle**—profitable in the short term but unsustainable for long-term author success.

Why Backlist Matters: The Algorithm's Long Memory

Amazon's algorithm does not only look at what is popular today—it considers **an author's cumulative data footprint**: total sales, average reviews, read-through rates across series, and how often readers return to that author. A strong backlist in a specific genre:

- Increases your **likelihood of being recommended** to genre-loyal readers,
- Improves the performance of **new releases** through "Also Bought" and follow-up marketing,
- Makes your brand **discoverable and trustworthy**, encouraging more sales from organic search.

Authors with consistent output in one or two adjacent genres often benefit from **algorithmic inertia**—a form of passive visibility that drives sales even without active promotion.

The Hybrid Strategy: Trend Hook + Evergreen Foundation

The most effective approach, therefore, is to blend **trending elements** with **evergreen appeal**. Rather than constructing a book entirely around a fleeting fad, authors can:

- Embed a current **trope or aesthetic** within a **timeless genre framework** (e.g., a mafia romance that still follows classic romantic pacing and character arcs),
- Set their book in a **reliably popular subgenre** (such as small-town romance, cozy mystery, or epic fantasy) but incorporate a currently popular reader hook,
- Ensure the book remains **structurally satisfying** even if the trend disappears (e.g., it still works as a standalone romance, not just as a TikTok aesthetic showcase).

This hybrid model allows authors to capture **early traction** via trend interest while preserving the book's viability as an **evergreen title**. Amazon often rewards such titles with long-term placements like:

- Inclusion in **"Classic in [Genre]"** or **"Recommended for You"** sections,
- Sustained **search ranking** due to steady conversion and good reviews,
- Ongoing visibility in **"Also Bought" loops**, especially if linked to other successful books.

Turning Trend Data Into Long-Term Leverage

When a trend-driven release performs well, it does more than just generate income—it **feeds data into Amazon's algorithm** that can boost your entire catalog. If readers enjoy your trend-aligned book, they may:

- Purchase or borrow other titles from your backlist,

- Sign up for your mailing list or follow your Amazon author page,
- Leave reviews that improve your author profile and book page conversion rates.

The algorithm takes note of this and often begins **surfacing your other books** to the same customer cohorts, especially if those titles share thematic or genre similarities.

Therefore, even a "flash-in-the-pan" success can become a **springboard for long-term discovery**—if it is backed by a catalog that is ready to catch the spillover.

Quality as the Sustainer of Visibility

Ultimately, no trend can compensate for poor reader satisfaction. If a book does not deliver on its promises—whether due to shallow characterization, poor editing, or underdeveloped plotting—readers will disengage. Amazon's algorithm notices:

- Low completion rates (especially for Kindle Unlimited),
- Negative reviews or low average star ratings,
- High return rates.

These signals weaken the book's long-term positioning, regardless of early hype. In contrast, a well-executed book that satisfies its audience may **continue selling well long after the trend has passed**, becoming a foundational title in your catalog.

Conclusion

In the KDP environment, **short-term trend alignment and long-term catalog building are not mutually exclusive—they are complementary.** A trend may provide the launchpad, but it is your backlist, brand consistency, and narrative quality that sustain momentum.

Use trends to your advantage—but build for longevity. By strategically incorporating popular themes into well-loved genre frameworks, and ensuring each release strengthens your author brand, you transform momentary attention into enduring success. **The algorithm will reward your spikes— but it will champion your consistency.**

VI

Reviews, Sales Velocity, Pricing, and Cover Design – Algorithmic Impacts

"Reviews, Sales Velocity, Pricing, and Cover Design – Algorithmic Impacts" explores the key external performance factors that signal value and drive visibility within Amazon's recommendation engine. "Reviews and Ratings" offer social proof and trigger increased algorithmic trust, while "Sales Velocity and Launch Momentum" play a pivotal role in boosting Best Seller Rank and recommendation placement. "Pricing Strategy", including Promotional Pricing, must balance conversion with profitability to optimize algorithmic exposure, especially in KU contexts like the KDP Select Global Fund. Elements like Dynamic Pricing and Testing help fine-tune this balance. Meanwhile, Cover Design and Click-Through Rate affect whether a book earns clicks in the first place. A compelling cover aligned with genre conventions (Genre Targeting with Cover) drives conversion, and Beyond the Cover, it's how all these signals interact that ultimately determines how—and how often—Amazon shows your book to readers.

26

Reviews and Ratings

Social Proof, Algorithmic Weight, and the Currency of Reader Trust

In the ecosystem of Amazon Kindle Direct Publishing (KDP), few elements exert as much influence on both consumer behavior and algorithmic visibility as **reader reviews and ratings**. They are simultaneously a form of **social proof for potential buyers** and a **critical data point for Amazon's recommendation engine**. Whether a reader is browsing casually or considering a targeted search result, the presence, volume, and tone of reviews play a substantial role in determining whether they will click, convert, and engage—actions which the algorithm watches with precision.

As Reedsy observes, **"When was the last time you bought a product with no reviews?"** This rhetorical question underscores a universal consumer impulse: people are drawn to what others have validated. For authors, reviews are not a vanity metric—they are a **strategic imperative**.

Reviews as Conversion Catalysts

At the most basic level, reviews **enhance trust**. A book with 40–100 positive reviews and an average rating above 4.0 is far more likely to convert a casual browser into a buyer or borrower. This increase in conversion rate is not just beneficial to the author's sales; it **directly influences the book's standing in Amazon's algorithm**.

Amazon tracks what percentage of shoppers **click and then buy**. If the presence of strong reviews boosts this percentage, the algorithm sees the book as high-performing for that search query or category—and subsequently **recommends it more often** via:

- "Customers Also Bought" carousels,
- "Highly Rated" filters in search results,
- Personalized marketing emails and browsing suggestions.

In this way, reviews operate as **a feedback loop**: they increase sales, which improves ranking, which improves visibility, which attracts more readers, which (ideally) leads to more reviews.

What the Algorithm Sees

While readers often parse the actual content of reviews, Amazon's algorithm focuses on **quantitative indicators**, including:

- **Total number of reviews,**
- **Average star rating,**
- **Ratio of verified purchase reviews,**
- **Reviews marked "Helpful" by other users,**
- **Frequency of new reviews** over time.

Importantly, **verified purchase reviews carry more algorithmic weight** than non-verified ones (SelfPublishingReview.com). They signal that the reviewer acquired the book through Amazon and is thus a legitimate customer. A book with dozens of verified five-star reviews is more likely to:

- Be considered for category feature placement,
- Appear in Amazon's "Highly Rated" lists (entirely driven by review metrics),
- Receive preference in keyword search results, particularly where competition is high.

This makes review cultivation not just a matter of reader engagement—but one of **algorithmic positioning**.

The "40+ Review Threshold": A Milestone of Credibility

Among experienced indie publishers, a common rule of thumb is to aim for **at least 40 reviews** early in a book's life cycle. Crossing this threshold provides several tangible and intangible benefits:

- It creates **critical mass**: a large enough review base that potential buyers feel reassured,
- It improves conversion metrics, which feed back into algorithmic ranking,
- It boosts the author's credibility in the genre space, leading to more organic discovery and word-of-mouth.

This milestone is particularly important for newer authors or books in competitive genres, where credibility and visibility must be established quickly to compete with more established titles.

Review Recency and Algorithmic Freshness

In addition to volume and rating, **recency matters**. A steady trickle of new reviews signals to Amazon that the book is still being read and remains relevant to current readers. This ongoing engagement helps:

- Sustain algorithmic visibility over time,
- Prevent stagnation in recommendation engines,
- Keep the book eligible for dynamic placements like "Trending Now" or "Popular Highlights."

Even one or two new reviews per month can serve as **algorithmic refresh signals**, indicating continued customer interest and satisfaction.

Cultivating Reviews: Ethical, Organic Strategies

While Amazon strictly prohibits incentivized or paid reviews, authors can ethically encourage reader feedback by:

- Including a **gentle review request** in the back matter of the book,
- Following up via **newsletter reminders** post-purchase or post-launch,
- Offering **Advance Reader Copies (ARCs)** to early fans, bloggers, or street teams with no obligation to review, but with encouragement to do so if they enjoy the book,
- Engaging authentically with readers on social platforms, where emotional investment often leads to voluntary reviews.

The goal is not just to increase volume, but to do so in a way that aligns with Amazon's terms and supports **long-term reader trust**.

Negative Reviews: Algorithmic and Behavioral Impact

Not all reviews are helpful. A pattern of negative reviews—particularly those that highlight unmet genre expectations, poor editing, or misleading marketing—can **erode both consumer trust and algorithmic favor**. Effects include:

- Lower conversion rates,
- Increased return rates,
- Decreased placement in recommendation engines.

While a few critical reviews can lend credibility (no book pleases everyone), a **swath of 1- and 2-star reviews** is a red flag to Amazon's algorithm that the book may not satisfy customers. In these cases, improvement in future editions, rewrites, or marketing clarity may be necessary.

Conclusion

Reviews and ratings serve as both **social proof to readers** and **performance signals to Amazon's algorithm**. Their influence on a book's commercial trajectory is outsized: they shape discoverability, conversion rates, and long-term visibility. Authors who understand this leverage reviews not only as feedback but as **a functional component of digital shelf optimization**.

Aim early for review credibility. Nurture ongoing engagement. Deliver a book worth recommending. If you build trust with your readers, the algorithm will follow their lead—and reward your book with the prominence it deserves.

27

Sales Velocity and Launch Momentum

Igniting Amazon's Algorithm for Maximum Visibility

In the Amazon Kindle Direct Publishing (KDP) ecosystem, **sales velocity—the speed and consistency with which your book sells—is one of the most powerful levers for algorithmic success**. Unlike traditional publishing, where books may have weeks or months to find their audience, Amazon's platform thrives on **immediate signals of demand**. When your book sells rapidly after launch—or maintains steady sales over time—the algorithm interprets it as a product in high demand, worthy of elevated placement, organic promotion, and sustained visibility.

This chapter explores how sales momentum affects your book's standing in Amazon's internal systems, how to generate that momentum, and why the **first 30 days post-launch** are often decisive for a book's trajectory.

Understanding Amazon's Best Seller Rank (BSR)

At the heart of Amazon's ranking system is the **Best Seller Rank (BSR)**, a rolling metric that **updates hourly** to reflect recent sales performance. As SelfPublishingReview.com explains, Amazon places **more weight on recent sales (especially within the last 24–48 hours)**, so a sharp spike in sales can cause a book's BSR to drop dramatically (remember, lower is better—#1 is the top spot). In practical terms:

- A sudden sales surge will immediately boost your BSR,
- A low BSR places your book **more prominently** in category charts and browsing lists,
- This visibility leads to **more organic sales**, which in turn reinforce your BSR in a feedback loop.

In short, **velocity drives visibility**, and visibility drives more velocity.

Launch Strategy: Building a Controlled Sales Surge

To capitalize on the algorithm's sensitivity to sales bursts, successful authors often **concentrate marketing and promotional efforts around launch week**. This strategic concentration has several objectives:

- Hit Amazon's **"Hot New Releases"** list (active during the first 30 days),
- Trigger the algorithm to place your book in **"Customers Also Bought," "Recommended for You,"** and **Amazon's marketing emails**,
- Push the book up category bestseller charts, which enhances visibility for weeks or months afterward.

As Reedsy advises, **"Big book sales will ultimately come down to stellar marketing,"** and one proven tactic is a **discounted launch promotion** (Blog.Reedsy.com). Pricing your book at $0.99 or $1.99 for a limited time can encourage more sales volume early on, especially if paired with coordinated outreach such as:

- **Newsletter swaps** with other authors in your genre,
- An **ARC (Advance Review Copy) team** committed to reviewing and spreading the word at launch,
- Scheduled **social media promotions**, giveaways, or BookBub feature

deals.

These efforts create the desired **sales spike** that Amazon recognizes as a sign of a "hot" book, which triggers further algorithmic attention.

The Power of Pre-Orders and Day-One Velocity

Another important tactic for maximizing sales velocity is **leveraging pre-orders**. Amazon counts **all pre-order sales toward Day-One performance**, meaning a well-marketed pre-order campaign can set your book up for a powerful debut.

According to Blog.Reedsy.com, **pre-orders accumulate momentum quietly**, but **on release day, they convert into a single-day surge**, instantly impacting your BSR and increasing the chances of landing on:

- **Hot New Releases** charts,
- **Genre-specific top 100 rankings**,
- Algorithm-driven emails and homepage features.

This tactic is particularly useful for authors with existing mailing lists or fanbases, as even a modest number of pre-orders (50–200) can provide a competitive edge at launch.

Sustained Sales: Staying Power Over Time

While a strong launch is essential, **Amazon's algorithm also rewards consistency**. Books that **continue to sell steadily**—even if modestly—are more likely to remain in recommendation loops. As Canopy Management notes, **"Sales rank is indicative of high customer demand,"** and Amazon naturally favors products that demonstrate **ongoing buyer interest**.

To sustain momentum after launch:

- Schedule **follow-up promotions** (e.g., price pulses, new ad campaigns)

in weeks 2–4,
- Release the **next installment in a series** quickly if applicable,
- Use **email list re-engagement campaigns** to keep your audience active,
- Consider enrolling in **Kindle Unlimited**, where page reads also count toward ranking.

This prolonged attention gives the algorithm additional data to keep your book in its internal promotion cycles well beyond the initial surge.

Algorithmic Outcomes of Strong Sales Velocity

Books with high and consistent sales velocity are more likely to:

- Appear in **high-traffic locations** like "Hot New Releases," "Top in Category," and "Highly Rated",
- Be shown in **Amazon's recommendation engine**, including "Customers Also Bought," "Readers Also Enjoyed," and "You Might Like" carousels,
- Trigger **email recommendations** and "Popular in [Genre]" alerts to potential buyers,
- Earn the coveted **"Amazon Best Seller" badge**, which itself boosts conversion rates and credibility.

This creates a **self-sustaining feedback loop**, where early and mid-term sales generate long-term visibility and income.

Conclusion

In Amazon's KDP environment, **sales velocity is both a signal and a catalyst**. It tells the algorithm that readers are interested, and that interest prompts Amazon to promote the book more widely—resulting in even greater sales. Launch momentum, therefore, is not just desirable—it is foundational to algorithmic success.

By engineering a concentrated sales surge at launch (via pricing, pre-orders, reviews, and outreach) and then maintaining consistent sales through sustained promotion and audience engagement, authors can ensure that **Amazon notices their book, promotes it, and continues to recommend it long after launch week ends**.

In the digital storefront where visibility is everything, **sales speed and staying power are the twin engines of author success**.

28

Pricing Strategy

Influencing Consumer Behavior and Algorithmic Visibility in the KDP Marketplace

In the Amazon Kindle Direct Publishing (KDP) ecosystem, **price is more than a number—it's a signal.** It not only influences how potential readers perceive the value of your book but also plays a measurable role in how Amazon's algorithm prioritizes your title within its marketplace. A well-planned pricing strategy can **maximize conversions, optimize royalties, and enhance your book's discoverability**, especially when synchronized with promotions, audience targeting, and launch momentum.

This chapter examines how pricing affects both **consumer psychology and algorithmic behavior**, and offers strategic frameworks for setting and adjusting your price point to best serve your sales goals.

Price and the Algorithm: A Revenue Optimization Loop

Amazon's algorithm is designed to **maximize platform-wide profitability**. While some believe it favors the lowest-priced content, the reality is more nuanced. The algorithm evaluates **conversion rate, sales volume, and revenue generation per session**, and it adjusts rankings and recommendations accordingly.

- A **lower price** may generate more units sold, improving conversion rates and reader volume.
- A **moderate or higher price**, if accompanied by steady sales, may deliver **higher net revenue** per customer interaction.
- Amazon's system dynamically analyzes these trade-offs and rewards books that demonstrate **efficient monetization of user interest**.

Thus, pricing is not static—it's a **performance variable** that influences your visibility and future placement across Amazon's recommendation engines.

Price as a Positioning Tool

Your book's price also signals its **market positioning**. Consumers use pricing cues to form expectations about quality, genre norms, and value:

- **$0.99 – $1.99**: Often used for promotional launches or loss leaders in series. These prices lower the barrier to entry and are ideal for capturing volume or initiating read-through.
- **$2.99 – $4.99**: The pricing "sweet spot" for many indie eBooks, offering a balance between perceived quality and affordability. This tier also qualifies for Amazon's **70% royalty rate** in most regions.
- **$5.99 and above**: Indicates premium content, longer works, or established author status. Works best with strong author branding or for non-fiction where readers are accustomed to paying more.

Setting an appropriate price helps attract the **right audience** and impacts how effectively Amazon can convert impressions into sales, which in turn improves algorithmic visibility.

Strategic Discounting: Driving Sales Velocity and Algorithmic Signals

One of the most effective ways to manipulate the algorithm is through **time-limited price drops**. Temporary discounts—especially during launch or promotion weeks—can rapidly increase sales volume and trigger improved rankings.

Key discounting tactics include:

- **KDP Select's Kindle Countdown Deals** (for eligible books): Allows authors to offer a book at a temporary discount while retaining the 70% royalty rate.
- **Free Promotions** (also via KDP Select): Useful for driving thousands of downloads, building reviews, or launching a series (especially Book 1).
- **Price pulsing**: Temporarily dropping a book to $0.99 or $1.99 during a promotional window, then returning it to a higher price afterward.

These methods, when coordinated with **email list promotions, ad campaigns, or newsletter swaps**, can result in a burst of sales velocity—**one of the key signals Amazon's algorithm uses to increase your book's visibility** in recommendation carousels and bestseller lists.

Series Pricing: The Funnel Approach

For authors publishing a series, pricing strategy often follows the **funnel model**:

- **Book 1: Free or $0.99** to remove friction and attract new readers.

- **Books 2 and 3: $2.99 – $4.99** to convert interest into revenue.
- **Later books: Premium pricing** (e.g., $4.99 – $6.99), as loyal readers are more price-tolerant once emotionally invested.

This approach works particularly well in Kindle Unlimited (KU), where read-through generates page reads and revenue regardless of the front-end price, and the algorithm rewards **repeat engagement and customer retention**.

Price Experimentation and Optimization

Amazon's system permits authors to **adjust their prices as often as needed**, enabling real-time testing of different pricing strategies. Key considerations include:

- **Monitoring your conversion rate**: If your product page receives traffic but few sales, price may be a barrier.
- **Watching sales rank movement** after a price drop: If BSR improves significantly, the discount is working.
- **Assessing royalty impact**: A lower price might increase unit sales but reduce net income if not carefully balanced.

The goal is to find the price that delivers **maximum revenue and sustained algorithmic traction**, which varies based on genre, book length, reader expectations, and author reputation.

Conclusion

Pricing is not just about revenue—it's about **positioning, discoverability, and long-term algorithmic performance**. In the KDP environment, the right pricing strategy can increase conversion, amplify visibility, and serve as a powerful trigger for the systems that govern Amazon's internal promotion. Whether launching a new title, optimizing a backlist, or designing a series funnel, authors should treat price as a **dynamic lever**—a strategic input that, when wielded effectively, boosts both profit and platform traction.

29

Conversion Rate vs. Per-Sale Value

Pricing Strategy and Algorithmic Weight in Amazon KDP

Among the most strategically significant yet often misunderstood decisions in self-publishing is **pricing**. In Amazon's Kindle Direct Publishing (KDP) ecosystem, your chosen price point not only influences **reader behavior** and **author earnings**, but also **how the Amazon algorithm interprets and promotes your book**. Striking the right balance between **conversion rate** (how many units you sell) and **per-sale value** (how much each sale earns and signals) is essential to maximizing both **visibility and profitability**.

This chapter explores how different pricing tiers affect your book's performance across Amazon's ranking systems—specifically Best Seller Rank (BSR), the lesser-known Popularity List, and recommendation algorithms—and offers guidance on how to sequence price changes to serve both short-term visibility and long-term sales sustainability.

Low Prices and the Conversion Advantage

Lower price points—particularly **$0.99 and $2.99**—tend to drive **higher unit sales**, especially during a book's launch window. These prices:

- Lower the barrier to entry for readers,
- Encourage impulse buys,
- Improve click-to-purchase conversion rates,
- Drive **sales volume**, which directly benefits **Amazon's Best Seller Rank (BSR)**.

As the **BSR algorithm** is largely governed by **raw unit sales** and Kindle Unlimited (KU) page reads, regardless of price, a flood of $0.99 purchases can quickly improve a book's BSR and help it:

- Appear on **bestseller lists within its categories**,
- Show up in "Hot New Releases" rankings,
- Benefit from higher visibility and more organic discovery.

Thus, many KDP authors adopt the **"low launch, high scale" model**: they launch a book at $0.99 to maximize visibility and BSR momentum, then raise the price later to capitalize on that visibility for more profitable sales.

Higher Prices and the Value Weight Advantage

While low prices may move more units, **higher-priced sales send a stronger signal in some of Amazon's deeper recommendation systems**. Notably, Amazon maintains a **hidden metric known as the "Popularity List"**, which is believed to weigh **revenue generated**, not just units sold.

As detailed by Reedsy, **"a $0 purchase (free) counts far less than a $2.99 sale, which counts less than a $9.99 sale"** in this popularity-based algorithm (Blog.Reedsy.com). In other words:

- BSR = Unit volume (price-agnostic),
- Popularity = Revenue-weighted (price-sensitive).

This distinction means that while a $0.99 book may rank high in BSR, a **$5.99 or $9.99 book with consistent sales** may outperform it in **recommendation carousels**, "Readers Also Bought," and other **algorithmically curated placements**. Higher prices suggest:

- Greater perceived value,
- Stronger reader commitment,
- Higher revenue for Amazon (a key performance metric from their perspective).

These factors may lead to increased algorithmic favor in discovery systems *beyond* BSR.

Strategic Price Sequencing: Best of Both Worlds

To reconcile these dynamics, many successful KDP authors implement **tiered pricing strategies** designed to capitalize on both the BSR benefits of high volume and the algorithmic "quality" signal of higher per-sale revenue.
   Common strategies include:

- **Launch at $0.99 or $2.99** for 5–7 days to build rank, reviews, and visibility,
- Then **raise to $3.99–$5.99** after hitting category charts and accumulating social proof,
- Occasionally **discount again** during promo cycles (e.g., Kindle Countdown Deals, BookBub features) to reinvigorate sales velocity.

This staged approach leverages the **high conversion rates of low pricing early on**, then transitions to a model where **each sale contributes more to your bottom line and popularity index**.

Note that this strategy works best in tandem with:

- A well-optimized product page (cover, blurb, categories),
- Early reader reviews (social proof),
- Coordinated launch and post-launch marketing.

Psychological Pricing and Reader Expectations

Beyond algorithmic implications, pricing also affects **reader psychology** and **genre expectations**. In certain genres, readers may interpret pricing as a signal of quality or genre alignment:

- Romance and cozy mystery readers often expect **$0.99–$3.99** books due to high consumption rates.
- Readers of literary fiction, historical nonfiction, or technical guides may expect **higher prices** and equate price with value.

Misaligning your price with genre norms can either deter buyers (too expensive) or signal poor quality (too cheap), thereby undermining conversion rates and damaging long-term reader trust.

The Risk of Free and Its Diminishing Returns

Free promotions (typically available only through KDP Select) can drive large download volumes and help with **review generation** or **email list growth**, but **free units count very little** in Amazon's deeper algorithms. While free books may appear in the **"Top 100 Free" lists**, they do not contribute meaningfully to BSR, popularity, or revenue-driven rankings.

Thus, while "free" can be an effective tool in limited, strategic contexts (e.g., the first in a series to drive read-through), it should not be confused with **sales velocity or ranking power** in the traditional sense.

Conclusion

Amazon's algorithm is sensitive to both **how many books you sell** and **how much revenue each sale generates**. Low prices improve conversion and boost short-term BSR; higher prices contribute more meaningfully to the algorithm's understanding of a book's market value and long-term appeal.

The most effective pricing strategy for KDP authors is therefore **not static but adaptive**: start low to ignite the algorithm, then shift to higher pricing to maximize profitability and solidify long-term visibility. This dual-focus approach leverages **both sides of Amazon's complex ranking systems**—volume and value—to achieve sustained success.

30

Promotional Pricing

Leveraging Deals to Trigger Algorithmic Momentum in Amazon KDP

In the Amazon Kindle Direct Publishing (KDP) landscape, one of the most potent tools available to authors—especially those enrolled in **KDP Select**—is **promotional pricing**. Used strategically, temporary discounts can act as algorithmic ignition switches, boosting **sales velocity, visibility, and long-term discoverability**. Whether through a Kindle Countdown Deal or a Free Promotion, authors can harness these promotions not merely to drive downloads, but to **manipulate Amazon's algorithmic attention**, pushing their books into high-traffic recommendation loops and bestseller lists.

This chapter examines how each type of promotional pricing works, how Amazon responds algorithmically, and how authors can build these tactics into an effective launch or backlist strategy.

Kindle Countdown Deals: Discount Without Sacrificing Royalties

Kindle Countdown Deals (KCD) are a powerful feature exclusive to KDP Select participants. They allow authors to **temporarily reduce the price of their book (as low as $0.99)** for up to 7 days, while still maintaining the **70% royalty rate** (on books normally priced between $2.99 and $9.99). This makes KCDs uniquely effective for **maximizing both volume and profit** during promotional periods.

But the true power of a Countdown Deal lies in its **algorithmic effect**. A well-timed countdown promotion can:

- **Spike your sales velocity**, which directly improves your Best Seller Rank (BSR),
- Qualify your book for placement on **Amazon's "Kindle Deals" page** and category-specific deal carousels,
- **Create urgency** for readers ("Buy now—price increases soon!"), thereby improving your conversion rate.

According to Reedsy, these sales bursts signal to Amazon that your book is in demand, prompting **greater exposure in "Hot New Releases," "Top in Category," and "Customers Also Bought" loops** during and shortly after the promotion (Blog.Reedsy.com).

Best Practice: Use a 5- to 7-day Countdown Deal during launch week or a strategic backlist promo—particularly for the first in a series—to maximize visibility and create a sales spike that benefits the entire catalog.

Free Promotions: Volume Over Revenue

While free promotions do not count toward **paid BSR**, they serve an entirely different and equally valuable purpose: **volume acquisition** and **reader base expansion**.

Amazon allows KDP Select authors to offer their book for free for up to **5 days every 90-day enrollment period**. Though these downloads do not influence paid rankings directly, they do:

- Accumulate thousands of **downloads**, which can boost your book to the **Top 100 Free** lists (a valuable visibility engine),
- Attract **new readers** who may review the book or buy sequels weeks or months later,
- Feed into Amazon's **Popularity List**, a lesser-known ranking system that factors in **free download volume to some extent** (Blog.Reedsy.com).

Books that rack up significant free downloads (e.g., 5,000–10,000 copies in a multi-day promo) may be reindexed more prominently by Amazon once they return to paid status—especially if followed by a secondary promo or continued read-through in Kindle Unlimited.

Key Strategy: Offer Book One in a series for free for 2–3 days, pair it with a price drop on Book Two, and monitor paid sales in the weeks following. Free readers often convert to buyers of subsequent volumes once they've read and enjoyed the free book.

The Aftermath Effect: Algorithmic Residue

One of the most important aspects of promotional pricing is the **residual benefit** that follows a promotion. While the spike in sales or downloads may only last a few days, the **algorithm continues to promote books that have shown strong recent performance**, especially if:

- Reviews increase as a result of the promo,
- Sales or KU reads of related books go up,
- The book maintains a higher BSR or remains in recommendation loops post-promo.

This phenomenon—sometimes called the **"halo effect"**—is particularly pronounced when:

- A Countdown Deal transitions into a higher price but maintains a portion of its new visibility,
- A Free Promotion brings in readers who begin reviewing, recommending, or buying sequels over the following weeks.

These secondary and tertiary effects are not accidental; they are **integral to Amazon's data-driven promotional logic.** The system identifies books with sudden engagement spikes and continues testing their appeal by showing them to new customers. If the performance sustains (clicks, buys, KU borrows), the book remains in rotation.

Combining Deals With External Marketing

While Amazon will provide some visibility during promotions, **authors should not rely solely on organic traffic.** For maximum effect, promotional pricing should be combined with:

- **Newsletter announcements** to your mailing list,
- **Newsletter swaps** or cross-promotions with other authors,
- Paid **promo list sites** like Freebooksy, BookBub (if accepted), or Bargain Booksy,
- **Social media campaigns** or influencer outreach.

The greater the traffic influx during the discounted window, the more likely Amazon's algorithm will **register and respond to the surge**, extending your visibility beyond the promotional period itself.

Conclusion

Promotional pricing is not merely a marketing tactic—it is an **algorithmic trigger**. Whether through a Countdown Deal that drives a burst of paid sales or a Free Promotion that expands your reader base and primes your catalog for future monetization, these tools give authors the power to **orchestrate their own algorithmic acceleration**.

Used intelligently, with clear timing and post-promo planning, these strategies can push a book from obscurity into sustained discoverability, feeding Amazon the kind of performance data that leads to **higher rankings, stronger recommendations, and more consistent sales**.

31

KDP Select Global Fund (KU) and Pricing

KDP Select, Kindle Unlimited, and Strategic Pricing in a Subscription Economy

For authors enrolled in **KDP Select**, one of the most consequential pricing considerations emerges from a paradox: **Kindle Unlimited (KU) readers don't buy your book—they borrow it.** Yet for algorithmic purposes, **those KU downloads count just like sales**, influencing your visibility, Best Seller Rank (BSR), and even recommendation placement. Understanding this dynamic is essential for pricing effectively within Amazon's hybrid sales-and-subscription environment.

This chapter explores how pricing interacts with KU behavior, the psychology of perceived value, and how authors can leverage subscription economics to **maximize algorithmic favor while maintaining pricing power**.

The Mechanics of KU and the Global Fund

When a KDP Select book is enrolled in Kindle Unlimited, subscribers can **download it "for free"** as part of their monthly plan. The author earns not through list price, but through **pages read**, calculated as Kindle Edition Normalized Pages (KENP). These reads are funded by the **KDP Select Global Fund**, which Amazon distributes monthly among all KU-enrolled authors based on total pages read.

However, **from Amazon's algorithmic perspective**, KU downloads are **treated equivalently to sales for ranking purposes** (Blog.Reedsy.com). That means:

- A KU borrow **boosts your BSR** just like a paid purchase,
- KU activity **signals popularity**, triggering Amazon's recommendation engine,
- A title with high KU engagement is more likely to appear in **"Top in Kindle Unlimited," "Customers Also Read,"** and **genre-specific KU carousels**.

In this model, **pricing becomes a strategic variable—not a hard gate.**

Pricing High in KU: The Premium Positioning Strategy

Because KU readers pay nothing additional to download your book, your **list price is irrelevant to their purchase decision**. Whether your book is $0.99 or $9.99, a KU subscriber sees "Read for Free." This opens the door to **premium positioning**: authors pricing their KU-enrolled books at **$4.99, $5.99, or even higher**, betting that:

- KU readers will borrow regardless,
- The higher price may **signal higher quality** to non-KU shoppers,
- Each non-KU sale earns more profit when it does occur.

In practice, this strategy can work well, particularly in **high-read-through genres** like romance, fantasy, or thrillers, where the bulk of readership comes through KU. As long as **your borrow volume and page reads remain high**, Amazon's system is likely to continue promoting the book—**even if paid conversions are modest**.

The Risk: Conversion Rate Outside KU

However, this strategy is not without risk. If your book is **priced too high for the competitive landscape**, and a significant portion of your potential audience is *not* in KU, you may experience a **drop in paid conversion rate**. Amazon interprets this data with cold logic: if shoppers are clicking but not buying, it's a sign that **the book lacks market appeal at its price point**.

According to Book Boss Academy, **"Amazon will see a low conversion rate as 'customers don't want this,'"** and may **suppress your visibility** in both organic search and recommendation placements (BookBossAcademy. Medium.com). This means you must weigh:

- How much of your audience is KU-based,
- Whether your genre supports premium pricing,
- The strength of your book's value proposition (cover, blurb, reviews).

A well-positioned, well-reviewed book in a high-demand genre might support a $5.99 price tag. A debut with no social proof in a price-sensitive niche likely won't.

Best Practices for Pricing in KU

To optimize pricing while enrolled in KDP Select, authors should:

1. **Benchmark genre norms**: Use Amazon search and tools like K-lytics to see what successful KU books in your genre are priced at. Avoid deviating too far from these unless you have strong justification.

2. **Match price to perceived value**: High-quality covers, tight editing, and a compelling product page justify higher pricing. If your book lacks these, lower pricing may convert better—even in KU.

3. **Use price as a positioning tool**: Pricing at $4.99+ can signal professionalism or premium content. This can influence non-KU buyers' perception, while KU readers remain unaffected.

4. **Monitor conversion rates and adjust**: Track your clicks-to-sales ratio. If you're getting traffic but few sales (and few KU borrows), a price drop may be necessary to re-engage the algorithm.

5. **Combine pricing with promotions**: Use Kindle Countdown Deals or periodic sales to test elasticity and drive spikes in both paid and KU engagement.

Conclusion

In the Kindle Unlimited economy, **pricing takes on a dual identity**: it's simultaneously irrelevant (to KU borrows) and critical (to non-KU conversion and perceived value). Amazon's algorithm rewards **total engagement**—purchases, borrows, and pages read—so optimizing your price involves understanding not just profit margins, but how **readers behave in a subscription model**.

Price too low, and you risk undercutting your brand and revenue. Price too high without a KU base, and you may lose visibility entirely. But with the right balance—anchored in genre expectations, product quality, and audience behavior—**you can turn KU enrollment and strategic pricing into complementary engines of discoverability and profit**.

32

Dynamic Pricing and Testing

Using Price as a Lever to Optimize Amazon Algorithm Performance

In the data-driven marketplace of Amazon Kindle Direct Publishing (KDP), **price is not just a static label—it is a strategic variable.** Unlike traditional publishing, where pricing decisions are locked and inflexible, KDP allows authors to adjust their prices at any time. This flexibility enables independent authors to experiment, optimize, and evolve their approach in response to market behavior. The underlying reality is simple: **Amazon's algorithm responds to results, not rigid pricing philosophies.**

By treating pricing as a tool—not a rule—authors can find the "**sweet spot**" that maximizes visibility, conversion, and revenue. This chapter explores how dynamic pricing strategies, including free promotions, price cycling, and long-term testing, can be deployed to influence the algorithm and improve both short- and long-term performance.

Amazon's Pricing Flexibility: The Foundation of Testing

KDP allows you to change your book's price as often as needed, whether to:

- Align with **seasonal trends,**
- Support **promotional campaigns,**
- Match **genre standards,**
- Or simply test **market response.**

The algorithm does not penalize price changes. In fact, it **recalculates performance metrics dynamically**, meaning that if a price change improves your conversion rate or sales volume, your algorithmic standing may improve quickly as a result.

For this reason, many seasoned authors use **dynamic pricing cycles**, toggling between:

- **Introductory pricing** ($0.99–$2.99) during launch or promotions,
- **Standard pricing** ($3.99–$5.99) for long-term profitability,
- **Occasional deep discounts** (or permafree) on series openers to feed the rest of the catalog.

Each pricing phase serves a distinct purpose—and each produces different algorithmic signals.

The Power of Permafree in Series Marketing

One of the most enduring pricing strategies in series publishing is making **Book One permanently free** ("permafree"). While this book will no longer appear in the **paid rankings**, it can achieve high visibility in the **Top Free charts**, and more importantly, it serves as a **loss leader** to drive sales of the sequels.

The algorithm tracks **read-through behavior**, if not explicitly then implicitly, by observing:

- How many customers who download the free book go on to purchase Book Two,
- How those sales impact the BSR and visibility of Book Two and beyond.

If your free Book One drives meaningful downstream purchases, Amazon's system will promote the sequels more aggressively. Additionally, because free books often get downloaded in large numbers, they can:

- Land in many Kindle libraries,
- Generate **"Customers Also Bought" data**,
- Result in long-tail discoverability through recommendations.

This means even if you make no direct revenue from the free book, you are **buying exposure** with attention—and the algorithm responds to that attention when it leads to real sales further down your series.

Price Cycling and Strategic Discounts

Another key tactic is **price cycling**—regularly adjusting your price to test elasticity, refresh visibility, or stimulate lagging sales. Authors often alternate between:

- **$0.99 promotions** to regain momentum,
- **Full price returns** to restore profit margins,
- **Timed discounts** using tools like **Kindle Countdown Deals** to create urgency.

The value in this method is not only financial. Amazon's algorithm reacts to **positive changes in sales velocity**. If a temporary price drop causes sales to spike, your BSR improves, which in turn increases visibility. When the price returns to normal, your higher position can result in **ongoing residual sales**—especially if paired with:

- Review boosts,
- Ads running concurrently,
- Strong metadata alignment.

This is not about tricking the system—it's about **feeding the system with better performance data**.

Conversion Over Price: What the Algorithm Really Sees

Authors sometimes ask whether cheaper books rank higher. The answer, technically, is **no**—the algorithm does not explicitly rank low-priced books above high-priced ones. But it does prioritize **books that sell well and convert effectively**, and those two outcomes are often facilitated by smart pricing.

A **"reasonable" price** that aligns with reader expectations and delivers perceived value will:

- Encourage **more purchases**,
- Improve **conversion rates** from product page views,
- Trigger **positive algorithmic signals** (consistent sales, satisfied readers, verified reviews).

Amazon doesn't require you to underprice—it simply expects your book to **perform**. If a $5.99 title converts well, Amazon will reward it. If a $0.99 title struggles, it won't be promoted. Pricing only matters in relation to **how it influences buyer behavior**.

Continuous Testing and Adaptation

The best authors are not locked into a single price—they are data-informed and **willing to adapt**. They test new pricing models regularly and ask:

- Does a higher price deter new readers?
- Does a lower price lead to significantly more sales or reviews?
- Does this price signal professionalism or cheapness in my genre?

Tools like Amazon Author Central, Book Report, and even manual tracking of rank and sales data can provide useful insights into which price points yield the best results for your goals.

Conclusion

Pricing is not a set-it-and-forget-it decision—it is a **living, tactical component** of your publishing strategy. Amazon's algorithm is responsive, performance-based, and increasingly intelligent. It will adjust to your pricing choices as long as those choices lead to results: high conversion, steady sales, and reader satisfaction.

Whether you're experimenting with permafree strategies, running promotional sales, or simply seeking the ideal price point for your audience, the key is to remain flexible, observant, and reader-centric. In doing so, you transform pricing from a guess into a **precision instrument of visibility, revenue, and long-term success.**

33

Cover Design and Click-Through Rate

The Visual Trigger that Powers Algorithmic Discovery

In the highly competitive environment of Amazon Kindle Direct Publishing (KDP), your book's cover is not merely a visual accessory—it is the **first and most influential signal** to both potential readers and the Amazon algorithm. While the algorithm cannot interpret aesthetics or understand design choices in a human sense, it **relentlessly monitors reader behavior**—and that behavior begins with the cover. As Coverrater.com bluntly asserts: **"Amazon's algorithm doesn't care about your plot or prose... What the algorithm does care about – obsessively – is customer behavior. And this behavior starts with your cover."**

The cover, in this context, is a **conversion tool**, and its effectiveness is measured by one critical metric: **click-through rate (CTR)**. If users scroll past your book without clicking, Amazon interprets this as a lack of interest. But if your thumbnail consistently captures attention and garners clicks, the algorithm rewards you with **increased visibility, ranking, and recommendation exposure**. In short, **your cover is your algorithmic bait**—and its power should never be underestimated.

The Role of the Cover in the Amazon Ecosystem

Unlike a bookstore, where customers can touch and browse physical books, Amazon operates as a **search- and thumbnail-driven marketplace**. Your book is judged in fractions of a second based on its cover alone. This image appears in:

- Search result carousels,
- Category bestseller pages,
- Sponsored ads,
- "Customers Also Bought" and "Hot New Releases" sections.

In all of these, the **thumbnail cover is the first—and sometimes only—element a potential reader engages with**. If it fails to resonate, they scroll past. If it intrigues or reassures them (by genre signaling, emotional appeal, or quality), they click. That click is the data Amazon tracks.

Click-Through Rate: The Algorithm's Behavioral Litmus Test

Amazon's algorithm is a reactive, data-hungry system. It doesn't evaluate quality directly—it watches **how customers behave**. And one of the first behaviors it measures is CTR: how often users who see your book's thumbnail **click to view the full product page**.

According to Coverrater.com, internal performance data shows:

- Books with **CTR below 2%** almost never receive further algorithmic promotion.
- Books with **CTR above 5%** often enter a **positive feedback loop** of rising visibility and sustained exposure.

The process looks like this:

1. A compelling cover gets noticed and clicked.
2. Higher CTR signals to the algorithm that the book is **relevant and attractive**.
3. Amazon responds by **surfacing the book more often** (in more carousels, higher ranks, and more recommendations).
4. Greater exposure leads to more clicks, conversions, and sales.
5. The algorithm observes the sales velocity and further reinforces visibility.

This is the virtuous cycle of **CTR-driven discoverability**. And it all begins with the cover.

The Genre Signal: What a Good Cover Must Convey

To be effective, a cover must not only be visually appealing—it must also be **genre-appropriate**. Readers make snap judgments based on genre conventions, and deviation from these norms can severely harm CTR. For example:

- A **paranormal romance** cover should signal sensuality, mystery, and perhaps supernatural themes—typically with moody lighting and suggestive typography.
- A **cozy mystery** needs warmth, whimsy, and illustrative elements—not gritty realism.
- A **military sci-fi** novel requires bold, clean fonts, action-oriented imagery, and tonal consistency with well-known titles in the genre.

A cover that fails to communicate genre accurately will confuse readers, discourage clicks, and ultimately **undermine the book's performance regardless of its narrative quality**.

Cover Design and the Death Spiral

Just as a strong cover can fuel algorithmic ascent, a weak one can trigger **algorithmic decline**. If a book receives **low CTR**, the algorithm interprets it as irrelevant. It will begin to:

- Suppress the book in search and category results,
- Remove it from recommendations,
- Deprioritize it in marketing emails and visibility carousels.

This decline creates what Coverrater.com calls the "**death spiral of algorithmic invisibility.**" The book becomes harder to find, fewer readers click on it, and without intervention—such as a cover redesign, ad campaign, or metadata overhaul—**it may quietly fade into permanent obscurity**.

Testing and Optimization: Data-Driven Design

Because Amazon allows real-time tracking of ad CTR, sales rank, and impressions, authors can **A/B test** cover options by:

- Running Amazon Ads with different covers (if using a pen name or variant listing),
- Monitoring CTR over a defined time window,
- Comparing engagement across platforms (e.g., BookFunnel test pages, Facebook groups),
- Surveying newsletter subscribers for visual preference.

Even slight improvements in CTR—moving from 2.5% to 4.5%—can dramatically change a book's visibility trajectory.

Conclusion

Your cover is not just an artistic decision—it is a **behavioral catalyst**. On Amazon, it functions as your book's storefront, billboard, and sales hook, all in one. The algorithm does not understand aesthetics, but it **understands human response**—and that response starts with a click. Covers that drive strong click-through rates will receive more algorithmic favor, while those that fail to capture attention will quietly sink, regardless of how brilliant the prose behind them may be.

To succeed in KDP, treat your cover not as a final step, but as a strategic pillar. **It is the first signal in the chain of discoverability, and in Amazon's world, it may be the most important.**

34

Cover and Conversion

How Design Drives Trust, Sales, and Algorithmic Favor

The journey from visibility to purchase on Amazon is short—but critically fragile. Once your book cover earns a **click** in search results or a carousel, the next hurdle is **conversion**: will the shopper who lands on your product page go on to **buy** the book? Here, too, the cover plays a decisive role. It is not merely a click-magnet; it is also a **trust signal**, a genre marker, and a psychological contract between you and your reader. If it fails in this capacity, Amazon's algorithm will **detect and penalize** the resulting poor performance.

As Coverrater.com states plainly, **"A professionally designed cover signals quality and builds trust... Amazon's algorithm treats conversion rates as golden signals of product quality."** In the attention economy, trust must be earned in seconds—and your cover is the first ambassador of that trust.

From Click to Purchase: The Cover's Role in Post-Click Behavior

Once a potential reader clicks your book, they land on the product page. This page contains several elements:

- The full-size cover,
- The title and subtitle,
- The book description (blurb),
- Reviews and ratings,
- The "Look Inside" sample, if enabled.

While all of these contribute to the buying decision, **the cover remains visually dominant**, particularly on mobile devices, where Amazon prioritizes imagery in the layout. A **genre-appropriate, professional cover** does more than attract interest—it **reassures** the reader that they are in the right place.

For example:

- A **cozy mystery** cover with pastel colors, hand-drawn motifs, and whimsical fonts tells the reader: "Light, charming, and low-stakes—just what you expect."
- A **thriller** cover with stark typography, moody lighting, and foreboding imagery tells the reader: "Dark, intense, and fast-paced."

This match between **reader expectation and visual presentation** is crucial. It anchors the reader psychologically and increases the probability that they will **move from interest to purchase.**

Conversion Rate: The Algorithm's Quality Check

Amazon's algorithm closely monitors **conversion rate**—the percentage of people who view your product page and then buy the book. This metric is perhaps the **single most important behavioral signal** Amazon tracks after click-through rate (CTR). It provides the algorithm with a clear message: "Do shoppers who find this book actually want it?"

As BookBossAcademy.Medium.com explains, **if people click but don't buy**, the algorithm concludes that something is off—perhaps the cover overpromised, the blurb was weak, or the overall package did not meet expectations. The result? **Deprioritization**. Amazon stops showing the book for key search terms or reduces its visibility in carousels.

Consider two books:

- Book A: 100 product page views → 25 sales = 25% conversion rate.
- Book B: 100 views → 3 sales = 3% conversion rate.

Amazon will **amplify Book A** because it's clearly appealing to the target audience. Book B, despite equal exposure, may get **down-ranked**, not because of poor writing—but because the **packaging failed to convert interest into action**.

Cover as Conversion Catalyst: Trust, Tone, and Promise

A strong cover works hand-in-hand with your title and blurb to establish **trust**. It tells the prospective buyer:

- This book belongs to a genre you know and love.
- It was created professionally—so the content likely reflects similar care.
- It is targeted at you—the reader Amazon has brought here through data and behavior.

Readers are often wary, especially when discovering new authors. A well-crafted cover that adheres to genre conventions (without being derivative) can **overcome that hesitation**. It confirms the reader's instincts and increases the likelihood that they'll move forward with the purchase or Kindle Unlimited borrow.

This is why cover design is not merely cosmetic. It is **a conversion tool and a signal amplifier**.

Early Performance and the Algorithm's Judgment Window

Amazon gives new books a brief period of **heightened algorithmic observation**—usually the first 30 days, and particularly the first 7–10 days. In this window, it evaluates:

- CTR from search results and ads,
- Conversion rates on product pages,
- Review momentum and reader response.

If a book performs well—high clicks and high conversion—it begins ascending in visibility. If it underperforms, **Amazon deprioritizes it rapidly**. As BookBossAcademy explains, "If it isn't getting clicks or purchases, Amazon has no reason to push that book on results pages."

The implication is clear: **you only get one chance at a first impression**, and your cover plays a pivotal role in shaping both the click and the purchase decision. A poor cover compromises both.

Don't Skimp on Design: Long-Term ROI

Given the central role of the cover in both **CTR and conversion**, it is economically irrational to underinvest in it. Authors who attempt DIY design or opt for generic templates to save money often **pay the price in algorithmic suppression** and lost sales.

Investing in a professional designer who understands:

- **Genre expectations,**
- **Market positioning,** and
- **Thumbnail legibility**
- is not an expense—it is **an algorithmic investment**.

Authors who treat their covers with strategic importance are far more likely to see:

- Improved ad performance (lower CPC due to higher engagement),
- Increased organic discovery,
- Stronger long-term sales velocity.

Conclusion

On Amazon, **your cover is the keystone of your conversion architecture**. It influences not just who clicks, but who buys—and the algorithm is watching both. A compelling, genre-aligned cover tells the reader that your book is relevant, professional, and worth their time. It boosts conversion rates, which Amazon interprets as confirmation of quality and reader interest.

Ignore your cover at your peril. But if you prioritize it—designing with strategy and reader psychology in mind—you not only attract more buyers but also earn the trust of the algorithm. And in the world of digital publishing, **trust is visibility.**

35

Genre Targeting with Cover

Aligning Visual Identity for Algorithmic Precision and Audience Fit

In the competitive ecosystem of Amazon Kindle Direct Publishing (KDP), the importance of cover design extends far beyond aesthetic appeal or marketing psychology. Emerging evidence, including disclosures from former Amazon insiders, suggests that **Amazon's algorithmic infrastructure actively uses cover images to help classify a book's genre** and determine which audiences are most likely to engage with it. In other words, your cover doesn't just affect human perception—it informs machine learning decisions as well.

This revelation fundamentally shifts how authors should approach visual design. A cover that fails to clearly signal its genre doesn't just risk alienating readers—it may also result in **algorithmic misclassification**, leading to mismatched recommendations, low engagement, and reduced visibility. As Coverrater.com notes, "The algorithm might actually get 'confused' if your cover broadcasts the wrong genre." This confusion translates directly into **algorithmic inefficiency** and poor commercial performance.

The Algorithm Reads Your Cover – Visually, Not Semantically

While Amazon's algorithm does not interpret plot, prose, or narrative quality, it is increasingly capable of parsing **visual patterns**—a capability central to image recognition models used across its platform. As revealed by a former Amazon product manager, **the system includes cover image analysis in its genre prediction process** (Coverrater.com). This visual classification is not semantic (i.e., it doesn't know what your book is about), but **pattern-based**. It detects:

- **Color schemes** associated with certain genres (e.g., pastels for romance, greyscale for literary fiction),
- **Font types and hierarchy** (e.g., serif for historical fiction, sans-serif for thrillers),
- **Imagery and layout styles** commonly found in genre clusters.

If your book's cover deviates from these genre signals, the algorithm may **misidentify your book's intended audience** and test it with the wrong one. This can quickly lead to low click-through and poor conversion, which in turn **devalues your book in Amazon's internal ranking systems**.

Misclassification and Its Algorithmic Consequences

The consequences of genre ambiguity in your cover are not speculative—they are **immediate and structural**. Consider a romance novel with a minimalist, text-heavy cover more akin to literary fiction. The algorithm may misread the genre, test the book with readers of contemporary or experimental lit-fic, and observe:

- **Low CTR (click-through rate)**: because the wrong readers are seeing the book,

- **Low conversion**: because even if they click, the content doesn't align with expectations,
- **High bounce rates** or return behavior: undermining Amazon's trust in the title.

The result is a **cascade of suppression**: your book gets fewer impressions in organic search, drops out of "Customers Also Bought" carousels, and may be excluded from genre-specific recommendations. This scenario is not a failure of writing, but of **visual misalignment**—one that the algorithm interprets as a failed product-market fit.

On-Brand Design: Aligning with Genre Expectations

To avoid these pitfalls and fully activate the algorithm's promotional potential, your cover must be **on-brand for your genre**. This doesn't mean copying competitors or producing generic art—it means designing with awareness of **visual cues that readers and machines alike recognize as belonging to your category**.

Essential cover components that must align with genre norms include:

- **Imagery and symbolism** (e.g., dragons in epic fantasy, weapons in thrillers, flowers or hands in romance),
- **Typography** (e.g., bold, capitalized fonts for action genres; flowing scripts for romance),
- **Color palettes** (e.g., warm pastels for cozy fiction, cold blues for sci-fi),
- **Composition and focal points** (e.g., character-centric vs. object-centric design).

Designing in line with these conventions helps **Amazon's algorithm accurately classify your book**, ensuring it appears alongside others in its category and reaches the intended audience. It also helps readers **instantly recognize genre alignment**, increasing trust and emotional resonance.

Visual Fit and Emotional Response: The Browse-to-Buy Effect

A genre-accurate cover not only aids classification—it also **accelerates decision-making**. When a shopper sees a cover that fits their expected genre aesthetic, their brain completes a familiar pattern: "This looks like the kind of book I enjoy." This psychological cue can significantly reduce "browse time" and shorten the path to purchase.

Amazon observes this as a **positive behavioral signal**. A faster browse-to-buy time suggests a strong product-market fit, which can result in:

- Increased conversion rate,
- Higher placement in search results,
- Greater likelihood of inclusion in personalized recommendation feeds.

In short, genre-aligned covers increase **both reader confidence and algorithmic confidence**. They make your book easier to sell—and easier for Amazon to sell for you.

Conclusion

Your cover is not just a creative asset—it is a **machine-readable genre signal**, a behavioral trigger, and a trust vector. By aligning your cover design with the visual conventions of your target genre, you enable both the **algorithm and the reader** to immediately understand what your book is and who it's for.

Deviation from genre norms may be a stylistic choice, but on Amazon, it comes at a cost: misclassification, reduced visibility, and diminished discoverability. Conversely, a cover that "fits" the reader's expectations helps the algorithm place your book with the right audience, generates higher engagement, and ultimately drives sales.

In the Kindle store, it's often said that readers judge books by their covers.

Increasingly, **so does the algorithm.**

36

Beyond the Cover

Optimizing the Full Book Package for Algorithmic and Consumer Engagement

In the digital marketplace of Amazon Kindle Direct Publishing (KDP), a successful book is not merely written—it is *packaged*. While the **cover** is the crucial first trigger for attention, it is only the first in a series of steps that must be executed with precision to convert interest into a sale. Every element on your Amazon product page—**title, subtitle, description, preview content, reviews, and additional enhancements**—contributes to a consumer's buying decision. And more importantly, **each of these elements is tracked and interpreted by Amazon's algorithm** through behavioral data such as click-through rate (CTR), conversion rate, and bounce rate.

As BookBossAcademy.Medium.com puts it: "Amazon's algorithm is ultimately trying to figure out what consumers are buying and what listings successfully attract those consumers." Your job as an author is to **build a product page that converts**, because high conversion rates translate into **algorithmic visibility, higher rankings, and sustained sales**.

The Product Page as a Sales Funnel

A best-practice approach is to view your product page as a **conversion funnel**, with each stage designed to **pull the customer closer to purchase**. The typical customer journey proceeds as follows:

1. **Cover** (visual gateway): Sparks interest from thumbnails or carousels.
2. **Title and subtitle**: Reinforce genre and value proposition.
3. **Book description**: Hooks attention, creates emotional resonance, and addresses reader expectations.
4. **"Look Inside" preview**: Provides proof of writing quality and narrative pull.
5. **Reviews and editorial blurbs**: Establish trust and social proof.
6. **Buy or borrow** decision: The conversion goal.

At each step, the algorithm is watching. If too many customers bounce at any stage—clicking but not buying, viewing but not engaging—it deems the book **less effective**, and over time, **reduces its visibility** in search results and recommendation engines.

Title and Subtitle: Clarity and Keyword Impact

Your **title and subtitle** are the first textual elements a shopper encounters. They must do two things:

- Clearly **convey the genre and tone** (e.g., "A Small Town Enemies-to-Lovers Romance" signals trope and audience),
- Optionally include **relevant keywords** for discoverability.

A confusing or overly vague title can reduce conversions by failing to signal alignment with reader expectations. Conversely, a strong, keyword-aligned subtitle can boost relevance in both **search indexing** and **emotional targeting**, increasing the likelihood of a click turning into a sale.

The Book Description: Selling Through Story and Structure

Once a shopper lands on the page, your **book description (blurb)** becomes the primary persuasion tool. This section is often underestimated but is central to whether a shopper moves forward.

A strong description should:

- Match the **emotional tone and genre promise** (e.g., suspense, romance, wit),
- Present **high-stakes questions** or intriguing character dynamics,
- End with a compelling **call to action** or open-ended hook,
- Use formatting (bold, line breaks, etc.) for **readability**.

From an algorithmic standpoint, this is content-neutral—**the algorithm doesn't read your blurb**—but its influence is profound: **it impacts conversion rate**, which the algorithm *does* track and weigh.

"Look Inside" Preview: Proof of Quality

The **"Look Inside" feature** gives shoppers a sample of your book's first pages—often the **make-or-break moment**. If the writing is polished, the pacing strong, and the opening hook engaging, the reader is far more likely to buy. However, if the sample contains:

- Typos or poor formatting,
- A slow or confusing start,
- Lack of clarity in point of view or structure,

then the shopper often exits, and your **conversion rate suffers**.

This is why the preview is not just a formality—it is a **critical performance zone**, and Amazon's algorithm reflects the behavior it triggers.

Reviews, Editorial Enhancements, and Trust Signals

While cover and content drive first impressions, **reviews solidify trust**. A book with 20–100 reviews and an average rating of 4.0 or above has a psychological edge—and a **conversion advantage**. In addition to customer reviews, authors can bolster the product page using:

- The **Editorial Reviews section** via Author Central (quotes from influencers, media, or review blogs),
- Author bio information that strengthens credibility,
- Notable accolades (awards, bestseller labels, blurbs from recognized figures).

These additions help reduce consumer hesitation and provide **affirmation that the book is a safe purchase**. Again, the algorithm isn't parsing the content of these endorsements—but it *is* monitoring the **behavior they influence**: more sales, more reviews, lower return rates.

The Feedback Loop: Engagement Breeds Visibility

When all elements of your product page work together—cover, title, description, preview, reviews—they form a **high-converting package**. This leads to:

- Higher **CTR** from search and carousels,
- Strong **conversion rate** on the product page,
- Increased **sales velocity** and/or KU borrows.

The algorithm watches these behaviors and **amplifies your book's exposure** accordingly:

- Moving it up search results,
- Placing it in genre-specific carousels,

- Featuring it in Amazon's recommendation emails.

This is the **positive feedback loop** at the heart of KDP success: **great packaging drives sales, sales fuel algorithmic visibility, visibility drives more sales.**

Conclusion

In Amazon's marketplace, the success of your book is inseparable from the quality of its **overall presentation**. While the algorithm itself does not interpret prose or artistic value, it reacts powerfully to **consumer behavior**, and that behavior is shaped by the **sequence of signals** your product page emits.

A weak title, poorly formatted preview, or generic description will undercut even a beautifully written book. A strong, aligned, and professionally designed package, on the other hand, will make the algorithm pay attention—not because it recognizes beauty, but because **it sees results.**

In a system where visibility is earned, not granted, **your packaging is your performance.** Treat every element—from cover to copy to layout—as part of a single, cohesive sales engine. Because when you optimize the totality of your book's presence, **Amazon takes notice—and so do your readers.**

VII

Algorithm-Driven Publishing: Mastering the Evidence-Based Strategies Behind Amazon KDP Success

"Algorithm-Driven Publishing: Mastering the Evidence-Based Strategies Behind Amazon KDP Success" presents a comprehensive framework for succeeding in the Kindle Direct Publishing ecosystem by understanding and leveraging Amazon's algorithmic logic. At its core is the **Amazon KDP Algorithm**, a system that favors books demonstrating strong engagement, consistent sales, and clear market alignment. Through **Evidence-Based Publishing**, authors can make strategic decisions rooted in data—such as reader behavior, search trends, and category dynamics—rather than guesswork. By **Mastering the Amazon KDP Ecosystem**, writers position their books not just for launch success, but for sustained algorithmic visibility and long-term discoverability.

Algorithm-Driven Publishing: Mastering the Evidence-based Strategies Behind Amazon KDP Success

37

Amazon KDP Algorithm

A Synthesis of Data, Strategy, and Reader Behavior

Amazon's Kindle Direct Publishing (KDP) ecosystem represents one of the most dynamic, data-driven marketplaces in modern publishing. For independent authors, mastering the platform is not simply a matter of uploading a manuscript and hoping for the best. Rather, it requires a deliberate understanding of how Amazon's algorithm—an evolving and opaque system—responds to **reader behavior, metadata optimization, sales performance, and market trends**.

Drawing from a wide body of industry expertise, author experiences, and platform data, this chapter synthesizes the most authoritative insights available on **how to work with Amazon's algorithm to maximize book visibility and sales**.

Ranking Inputs: What the Algorithm Monitors

As Ricardo Fayet of Reedsy explains in *Amazon Algorithms for Authors — Demystified!*, the algorithm primarily watches **customer behavior metrics**: click-through rate (CTR), conversion rate, sales velocity, and read-through (for KDP Select titles). Amazon's algorithm does not evaluate prose quality or narrative structure—it observes which books are **getting attention, being purchased or borrowed, and read through to completion** (blog.reedsy.com).

This performance-driven framework means that:

- A well-performing book earns increasing exposure through bestseller lists, "Hot New Releases," and "Customers Also Bought" carousels.
- A poorly converting listing—no matter how well-written—sinks into obscurity.

Genre Trends and Market Alignment

Self-Publishing School and Automateed both emphasize that Amazon's bestsellers are **concentrated in a few dominant genres**. Fiction-wise, **romance and thrillers** consistently perform best. On the nonfiction side, **self-help, business, biographies, and spirituality** dominate in Kindle sales volume (self-publishingschool.com; automateed.com). Writing in one of these categories provides the best chance of tapping into high-demand reader bases.

Dave Chesson at Kindlepreneur extends this with data on **emerging subgenre trends** and **search term spikes**—such as "romantasy," "academy fantasy," and "mafia romance"—which suggest Amazon's search algorithm is sensitive to **real-time market interest** (kindlepreneur.com). Books aligning with these terms are far more likely to be surfaced organically.

KDP Select and Kindle Unlimited: The Power of Page Reads

Enrollment in **KDP Select** unlocks eligibility for **Kindle Unlimited (KU)**, which expands your reach among subscription readers and influences ranking. KU borrows count toward Amazon's Best Seller Rank (BSR) in the same way as sales, and more importantly, **page reads drive author income and engagement metrics** (blog.reedsy.com).

Authors often report that KU reads comprise 50–70% of their total activity. Books that perform well in KU benefit from inclusion in **"Top KU Titles,"** **KU-specific carousels, and email promotions**, further compounding visibility.

Sales Velocity and Launch Strategy

Sales velocity—the number of copies sold in a short period—is one of the most potent ranking factors. As Matthew J. Holmes and SelfPublishingReview.com both note, **ranking is updated hourly**, with recent activity weighted heavily (matthewjholmes.com). A successful launch, particularly within the first 48 hours, can push a book into bestseller lists, triggering algorithmic promotion.

This underpins the popularity of the **"rapid release" strategy**, discussed widely in Reddit's r/selfpublish community: authors releasing books every 30–60 days keep momentum, feed the algorithm, and retain reader engagement.

Metadata: Keywords, Categories, and Positioning

Your metadata—title, subtitle, keywords, and categories—form the **foundation of discoverability**. According to Kindlepreneur, precise keyword selection can get a book indexed for **multiple subcategories** beyond those selected manually (kindlepreneur.com). Including search phrases like "enemies to lovers romance" or "space marine sci-fi" in metadata and descriptions helps Amazon match the book to relevant shoppers.

Moreover, **category selection** is not trivial. As Kindlepreneur's category guide emphasizes, choosing a narrow, low-competition category can dramatically increase the odds of earning a #1 **Best Seller badge**, which boosts conversion (kindlepreneur.com).

Cover Design and Conversion

CoverRater.com provides a critical insight: **Amazon's algorithm infers value from behavior, and behavior starts with the cover**. A strong, genre-aligned cover increases CTR; a poor cover suppresses it. Books with <2% CTR rarely receive algorithmic promotion, while those above 5% may enter a virtuous cycle of increased visibility (coverrater.com).

Equally, **genre-consistent design helps the algorithm classify the book correctly**, as Amazon uses image analysis to determine genre targeting (coverrater.com). A thriller with a cozy mystery aesthetic may be shown to the wrong audience, harming engagement metrics.

Product Page Optimization

The rest of the listing—title, description, preview, and reviews—functions as a **conversion funnel**, as emphasized by Book Boss Academy. Each element must guide the shopper toward purchase. Poor descriptions, typos in previews, or weak blurbs reduce conversion, signaling to Amazon that the listing is ineffective (bookbossacademy.medium.com).

Conversion rate (purchases per page view) is a **critical quality signal**. Books with low conversion see diminished visibility over time, even if initial CTR was strong. Conversely, books with high conversion remain prominent in search and recommendations.

Reviews and Algorithmic Confidence

Reviews act as social proof. According to Self-Publishing Review, books with **40+ verified reviews** see improved conversion and credibility. While Amazon does not read the text of reviews for ranking purposes, it tracks:

- Total number of reviews,
- Star rating average,
- Verified purchase status,
- "Helpful" votes (selfpublishingreview.com).

More positive, verified reviews translate into higher algorithmic confidence and broader exposure.

Promotional Tools and Pricing Strategies

Promotions—especially **Kindle Countdown Deals** and **free runs**—can generate sales spikes that feed the algorithm. Countdown Deals retain the 70% royalty and can place a book on Amazon's "Kindle Deals" page, attracting deal-hungry shoppers (blog.reedsy.com). Free promos don't contribute to paid BSR, but **massive download volumes can boost sequel sales** and generate reviews that support future ranking.

Pricing also impacts visibility: **lower prices drive higher volume and BSR improvement**, while **higher prices may improve algorithmic value in Amazon's "popularity" ranking**, especially for full-priced titles (blog.reedsy.com; selfpublishingreview.com).

The Holistic Strategy: Feedback Loops and Optimization

Ultimately, the KDP algorithm functions as a **performance-reactive system**. The elements it favors—CTR, conversion, page reads, and review quality—are all results of how well your book meets reader expectations. This means authors must **engineer a product that aligns with market norms**, from genre and cover to pricing and promotional cadence.

A well-positioned book will enter a **positive feedback loop**:

- High-quality packaging → more clicks → more purchases → higher ranking → more exposure → repeat.

Poorly optimized books, by contrast, get caught in a **downward spiral** of low engagement and algorithmic suppression.

Conclusion

Publishing success on Amazon is not luck—it is strategy, execution, and responsiveness to data. Authors who understand the mechanisms of Amazon's algorithm and optimize each component of their book's presence—cover, content, metadata, marketing—are far more likely to achieve visibility, sales, and sustained readership.

As the synthesis of these sources makes clear: **Amazon rewards what readers respond to. Build for them, and the algorithm will follow.**

38

Evidence-Based Publishing

How Key Sources Illuminate the Amazon KDP Algorithm

To navigate the Amazon Kindle Direct Publishing (KDP) platform success-fully, authors must understand more than just writing and publishing—they must grasp the mechanisms of discoverability, sales performance, and algorithmic promotion. Over the past several years, a range of thought leaders, data analysts, and publishing strategists have deconstructed the inner workings of Amazon's algorithm. This chapter presents a curated synthesis of those authoritative sources and the strategic principles they reveal.

Authoritative Industry Voices

Ricardo Fayet's "Amazon Algorithms for Authors — Demystified!" (Reedsy) provides a foundational framework for understanding how Amazon tracks and promotes books. Fayet outlines how the platform does not assess quality directly, but instead evaluates customer behavior through metrics such as click-through rate (CTR), conversion rate, sales velocity, and

Kindle Unlimited (KU) read-through. These signals guide the algorithm's decisions to surface books in search results, carousels, and curated emails. The implication is clear: success on Amazon is not about writing quality alone, but about consumer response.

Sales Trends by Genre

The **Self-Publishing School** offers compelling genre-specific insights. Romance and thrillers dominate in fiction, while self-help, business, and spirituality perform best in nonfiction. Similarly, the **Automateed 2024 Sales Report** confirms that nonfiction categories such as biography, self-improvement, and religious titles rank highly in Kindle e-book sales volume. These sources indicate that aligning your book with high-demand genres substantially increases its likelihood of algorithmic promotion.

Keyword and Category Targeting

Dave Chesson at Kindlepreneur has published multiple in-depth analyses on keyword selection and category optimization. His 2025 keyword trend report identifies surging subgenres—such as "romantasy," "academy fantasy," and "shifter romance"—demonstrating the power of trend alignment. Chesson also explains how strategic use of metadata, including keywords and backend categories, can place books into more visible, lower-competition niches, enhancing their chances of earning a bestseller badge.

Cover Design and Algorithmic Impact

According to **CoverRater.com**, cover design is one of the most powerful drivers of CTR—and, by extension, Amazon's algorithmic attention. A cover that clearly signals genre and matches reader expectations generates clicks and conversions. Conversely, misaligned or unprofessional covers reduce engagement, leading the algorithm to demote visibility. The platform also reveals that Amazon's image processing system uses cover art for **genre**

classification, meaning visual design affects both human and algorithmic understanding of your book.

Sales Velocity and Format Performance

Matthew J. Holmes, an experienced indie author and marketer, shares granular data on how format (eBook vs paperback vs KU reads) affects Amazon ranking. His blog reveals that eBooks—especially those read through KU—drive most indie author income and algorithmic movement. Holmes and others confirm that sales velocity (i.e., number of units sold in a short window) is heavily weighted in BSR calculations, making coordinated launch strategies and discounted promotions critical to visibility.

Conversion Rate and Listing Optimization

Christina Kaye at Book Boss Academy emphasizes that Amazon evaluates how effectively a book converts viewers into buyers. She likens the book's product page to a funnel: the cover must capture attention, the title and description must build interest, and reviews must reinforce trust. Low conversion rates signal to Amazon that your book isn't resonating, which results in suppression from search and recommendation features.

The Role of Reviews and Author Central

The **Self-Publishing Review** outlines how verified reviews and reader engagement improve your standing in Amazon's "Highly Rated" filters. It also explains that Amazon allows authors to enhance listings through Author Central tools—such as editorial reviews and custom author bios—which improve trust and conversion, especially among cold readers.

Author Discussion Forums and Anecdotal Trends

On **Reddit's r/selfpublish**, many authors discuss real-world tactics and confirm that **rapid release strategies** (publishing every 30–60 days) maintain algorithmic momentum. While anecdotal, these user-based insights align with observed performance data and platform behavior.

Conclusion

The sources presented above collectively demystify how Amazon's algorithm works—and what authors must do to thrive within it. From the moment a reader sees your cover to the final click on the "Buy Now" button, every behavioral signal they emit is captured, analyzed, and fed back into Amazon's promotion system. Understanding and leveraging this process is what separates hobbyists from professionals.

The lesson is simple but unrelenting: what readers respond to, the algorithm promotes. Armed with this evidence, authors can design their publishing strategies not around hope, but around what *works*—informed by data, reinforced by practice, and driven by insight.

39

Mastering the Amazon KDP Ecosystem

A Cross-Source Synthesis of What Truly Drives Visibility and Sales

The Amazon Kindle Direct Publishing (KDP) marketplace is governed not by guesswork or chance, but by a set of algorithmic responses to author choices and reader behavior. To navigate this system successfully, an author must not only understand the inner workings of Amazon's infrastructure but also synthesize the best evidence and advice from experienced professionals, data analysts, publishing strategists, and the broader author community.

This chapter distills findings from the industry's most respected sources to create a coherent, actionable framework that KDP authors can use to improve their book's discoverability, market positioning, and long-term viability.

Reader Behavior is the Algorithm's Compass

Amazon's algorithm is not sentient—it does not read your prose or evaluate your storytelling. As explained repeatedly by **Reedsy**, **Book Boss Academy**, and **SelfPublishingReview**, what it does monitor—obsessively—is **reader**

behavior. Metrics such as:

- Click-through rate (CTR),
- Conversion rate (from product page view to sale or borrow),
- Sales velocity,
- Kindle Unlimited (KU) page reads,
- Review volume and quality,

are all converted into performance signals. These signals, in turn, dictate whether your book is pushed forward via Amazon's recommendation engines, search prioritization, bestseller lists, and marketing emails.

Cover Design: The First and Most Crucial Gatekeeper

The cover is the visual trigger that initiates all downstream engagement. According to **CoverRater**, CTR below 2% often dooms a book to algorithmic suppression, while CTR above 5% can initiate a promotional feedback loop. Your cover must:

- Match genre conventions,
- Clearly signal your book's thematic and emotional promise,
- Be legible and compelling as a thumbnail.

Moreover, the **algorithm uses cover imagery for genre classification**, meaning off-brand design choices can result in miscategorization and poor targeting.

Metadata Is Mission-Critical: Keywords, Categories, and Titles

Kindlepreneur highlights how smart use of keywords and subcategories can extend a book's visibility across the Amazon store. KDP allows up to 7 keyword fields, and those should include **searchable, reader-driven phrases** that reflect tropes, tone, and genre (e.g., "small town clean romance," "alien invasion sci-fi," "psychological thriller").

Properly chosen **categories**—especially niche ones—can drastically lower the threshold required to hit bestseller status. As **SelfPublishingReview** and **Reedsy** emphasize, bestseller tags, once achieved, act as social proof and influence both the algorithm and reader perception.

Pricing and Promotions: Triggering Visibility with Strategy

According to data from **Matthew J. Holmes**, **KDP Community**, and **Book Boss Academy**, most indie authors see 70–90% of their revenue come from eBooks—particularly in KU. This dynamic makes price flexibility an essential tool. Authors routinely:

- Launch at $0.99 to boost sales velocity,
- Transition to higher price points after securing visibility,
- Use **Kindle Countdown Deals** to drive urgency without sacrificing royalties,
- Occasionally make Book 1 of a series **permafree** to feed sequels and build read-through.

Reedsy and **Canopy Management** further reinforce that Amazon's hourly-updated Best Seller Rank (BSR) rewards recent activity—meaning that promotional bursts can have outsized impact if properly timed.

Kindle Unlimited and Read-Through Value

Enrollment in **KDP Select** grants access to **Kindle Unlimited (KU)**, which is the backbone of many authors' income. As **Reedsy**, **Matthew J. Holmes**, and **Book Boss Academy** explain, KU borrows and page reads are weighted equally to sales in BSR and algorithmic assessment.

Crucially, Amazon observes **whether readers go on to read sequels**. Therefore, series writing—paired with a strong Book 1—is algorithmically rewarded. This is why the **Reddit self-publishing community** emphasizes series and rapid release schedules as long-term visibility strategies.

Conversion Optimization: Every Page Element Matters

Book Boss Academy, **CoverRater**, and **SelfPublishingReview** urge authors to treat their Amazon product page as a **conversion funnel**. Once a reader clicks the cover:

- The **title** and **subtitle** should reinforce genre and entice curiosity.
- The **description** must hook attention and affirm reader expectations.
- The **"Look Inside" preview** must immediately demonstrate quality.
- **Verified reviews** and **Author Central enhancements** (editorial blurbs, awards) complete the sale.

Amazon's algorithm observes whether viewers exit the page without purchasing. High bounce rates and low conversion rates result in **demotion from search rankings and "Also Bought" lists**.

Reviews and Social Proof: Long-Tail Success Indicators

Amazon tracks **review volume**, **average star rating**, and whether reviews are **verified purchases**. According to **SelfPublishingReview** and **Book Boss Academy**, books with 40+ reviews tend to convert more effectively and gain more algorithmic favor. Verified reviews are more valuable, as they signal genuine reader engagement.

Market Awareness and Trend Alignment

Kindlepreneur, **Self-Publishing School**, and **Automateed** all demonstrate that being in the right genre—and capitalizing on emerging subgenres—can drastically influence discoverability. Readers currently seek out genres like:

- "Romantasy" (romantic fantasy),
- "Cozy mystery,"
- "LitRPG" and "shifter romance."

Writing to market doesn't mean formulaic storytelling—it means writing stories that already have hungry audiences.

Conclusion: Synthesis into Strategy

The KDP marketplace rewards books that are **visually compelling, precisely positioned, and behaviorally successful**. Your strategy should reflect a feedback-aware mindset:

- **Strong first impression (cover, title)** → high CTR,
- **Compelling product page (blurb, preview)** → high conversion,
- **Series design and pricing strategy** → high read-through and long-term revenue.

From clicks to reviews, every interaction a reader has with your listing is logged, assessed, and acted upon. Each favorable engagement boosts your discoverability, and each misstep dampens it.

By integrating the findings from these respected sources, authors can stop guessing and start **publishing with precision**.

40

Conclusion

The contemporary publishing ecosystem is no longer defined solely by editorial discernment, literary gatekeeping, or institutional affiliation. Instead, it is increasingly governed by algorithmic architectures that filter, rank, and recommend content based on data-driven metrics of performance and engagement. Amazon Kindle Direct Publishing (KDP) exemplifies this shift, functioning as both a democratizing platform and a competitive algorithmic marketplace in which authors must navigate visibility through strategic design rather than traditional literary validation.

This study has examined the core determinants of success within the KDP ecosystem, identifying the key factors that influence algorithmic promotion and discoverability. Among these are genre selection, metadata optimization, pricing strategies, cover design, reader reviews, and Kindle Unlimited engagement—all of which form a matrix of inputs that Amazon's recommendation systems evaluate in real time. Importantly, these mechanisms are not neutral. They reflect and reinforce prevailing consumer preferences, privileging high-volume, high-engagement titles while marginalizing outliers, experimental genres, and content with niche appeal.

While KDP has enabled a vast expansion of literary participation—empowering authors from diverse backgrounds to publish and distribute their work globally—it has also instituted new pressures. Success is increasingly contingent upon understanding and adapting to algorithmic logic. The concept of "writing to market" and the strategic manipulation of metadata are now integral to the authorial process, blurring the boundaries between creative production and platform optimization.

Yet this convergence should not be understood as wholly deterministic. As this book has argued, authors retain agency—not in circumventing the system, but in mastering it. A critical literacy in algorithmic dynamics, coupled with a principled approach to content creation, offers the best path forward for independent authors seeking both visibility and integrity in a platform-dominated environment.

Ultimately, the question is not whether authors should engage with Amazon's algorithmic infrastructure, but how they can do so in ways that are informed, intentional, and sustainable. The tools exist, the data is available, and the systems—while opaque—are not unknowable. By embracing both the art and science of digital publishing, authors can reclaim a measure of control within an ecosystem that is, paradoxically, both open and constraining.

This book has offered a roadmap toward that end—an attempt to make legible the algorithmic forces shaping literary circulation today. The future of publishing will undoubtedly evolve, but the imperative remains constant: to write, to adapt, and to persist within and beyond the logic of the platform.

Epilogue

The emergence of Amazon Kindle Direct Publishing marks more than a technological milestone; it signals a fundamental reconfiguration of authorship, readership, and the mediation of literary value. What once required the institutional scaffolding of traditional publishing—agents, editors, print distribution networks—can now be accomplished through a laptop, an internet connection, and a knowledge of algorithmic behavior. But this newfound access does not come without cost.

This work has shown that the infrastructure of self-publishing is, at its core, algorithmic. Visibility is not determined solely by content or craft, but by metadata fields, pricing thresholds, genre conventions, and reader behavior metrics. Algorithms now serve as the de facto gatekeepers, shaping which narratives are elevated and which remain unseen. This mechanization of literary circulation reorients the role of the author toward that of a hybrid: equal parts creative, strategist, and data-literate participant in a dynamic platform economy.

And yet, there is promise in this paradigm. The tools of publishing are now within reach of anyone willing to understand them. The algorithms, while complex, are not impervious to analysis. They respond to signals—reader engagement, conversions, completion rates—that authors can influence through intentional design and authentic connection. The opportunity, then, lies not in resisting these mechanisms, but in mastering them without losing sight of the fundamental aim: to create meaningful work that resonates with others.

In the evolving landscape of digital authorship, power resides with those who adapt. And while the future of publishing will continue to be shaped by platform economics and computational logic, the enduring relevance of storytelling, inquiry, and human expression remains unshaken. To write today is to enter into dialogue with both algorithms and audiences—and in that space, new forms of literary agency can be forged.

Afterword

As the final pages of this work are written, it is evident that the questions posed by the rise of Kindle Direct Publishing and algorithmic gatekeeping are far from settled. This study has sought to clarify the operational mechanisms by which books are discovered, elevated, or neglected in the largest self-publishing ecosystem in the world. Yet the system itself remains in flux, subject to continual revision by technological shifts, platform policy changes, and evolving reader behavior.

If there is a central lesson to be drawn from this inquiry, it is that authorship in the digital age cannot be disentangled from platform literacy. The process of writing no longer ends at the final sentence of a manuscript; it extends into the architecture of metadata, the cadence of content marketing, and the responsiveness to algorithmic trends. What was once a solitary act of creation is now a complex negotiation with market forces governed, in large part, by automated systems.

Nonetheless, this new terrain is not inherently inimical to authors. Indeed, it offers possibilities that were previously unimaginable: instant global distribution, direct audience engagement, and control over the full lifecycle of a work. These are profound affordances. But they demand of the author a new kind of discipline—one grounded not only in craft, but in strategic awareness.

This book concludes with a reaffirmation of the value of knowledge in navigating systems of power, even those embedded in code. To understand how the KDP platform functions is not merely to optimize one's commercial prospects—it is to reclaim a degree of autonomy in a world where visibility is increasingly engineered. The future of independent publishing belongs to those who treat the algorithm not as an obstacle, but as a structure that can be studied, understood, and ethically engaged.

Sources

1. From Manuscript to Bestseller: How Your Book Cover Influences Amazon's Algorithm | CoverRater.com
2. The Most Popular Book Genres on Amazon Revealed
3. 2024 Amazon Book Sales Statistics: Insights & Trends
4. Most Searched Amazon Keywords & Trends (2025 Update)
5. Mastering the Amazon KDP Algorithm to Increase Book Sales! | by Christina Kaye | Medium
6. Amazon Algorithms for Authors — Demystified!
7. Your ratios of ebook vs. paperback sales? - KDP Community
8. Matthew J Holmes | Amazon Ads: Kindle vs Paperback Format
9. Wait until the series is done, or publish one at a time? - Reddit
10. Mythbusting The Amazon Algorithm – Reviews and Ranking For Authors | Self-Publishing Review
11. Amazon Book Categories SECRETS: [READ before choosing!!!]
12. Decoding the Amazon Algorithm: 10 Things Amazon Sellers May …

About the Author

Abdellatif Raji is an independent scholar and autodidact with a sustained commitment to the critical study of digital publishing systems, algorithmic governance, and the evolving role of authorship in the platform economy. Operating outside the boundaries of formal academic institutions, his expertise has been cultivated through extensive self-directed research, critical engagement with interdisciplinary scholarship, and applied experience within the Kindle Direct Publishing ecosystem.

Drawing upon both theoretical frameworks and empirical observation, Raji analyzes the intersection of literature, technology, and market infrastructure. His work reflects a nuanced understanding of how algorithmic mechanisms influence discoverability, reader behavior, and the circulation of knowledge in digital environments.

As an autodidact, he embodies the principle that rigorous intellectual inquiry need not depend on institutional validation. Through his writings and research, Abdellatif Raji contributes meaningfully to contemporary discussions on digital authorship and demonstrates that independent scholarship can meet—and in many cases exceed—the standards of traditional academia.

You can connect with me on:

🌐 https://www.abdellatifraji.com

Subscribe to my newsletter:

✉ https://www.amazonkdpalgorithm.com

www.ingramcontent.com/pod-product-compliance
Lightning Source LLC
Chambersburg PA
CBHW030934220326
41521CB00040B/2313